TWAYNE'S WORLD AUTHORS SERIES

A Survey of the World's Literature

SPAIN

Janet W. Díaz, University of North Carolina, Chapel Hill

EDITOR

Gabriel Celaya

TWAS 483

Gabriel Celaya

GABRIEL CELAYA

By SHARON KEEFE UGALDE

Southwest Texas State University

TWAYNE PUBLISHERS
A DIVISION OF G. K. HALL & CO. BOSTON

Library of Congress Cataloging in Publication Data

Ugalde, Sharon Keefe.
  Gabriel Celaya.

  (Twayne's world authors series ; TWAS 483 :
Spain)
  Bibliography: p. 151–57
  Includes index.
  1. Múgica, Rafael—Criticism and interpretation.
PQ6623.U34Z9   861'.6'4   77-26236
ISBN 0-8057-6324-4

To My Parents
Otho and Betty Keefe

Contents

About the Author

Sharon Keefe Ugalde studied at the University of California at Davis and at the University of Madrid. She received her Ph.D. in Spanish from Stanford University in 1973 and at present is Assistant Professor of Spanish at Southwest Texas State University.

Professor Ugalde's previous publications have appeared in *Papeles de Son Armadans*, *Revista de estudios hispánicos*, and *Hispania*.

Preface

Gabriel Celaya is perhaps the most strident and forceful of the first group of young Spanish poets to begin writing after the Spanish Civil War (1936–1939). His poetry is historically important because he was living and writing in Spain at a time when literature struggled to survive under the repressive dictatorship of Francisco Franco. Celaya is best known for his outspoken support of social poetry, going so far as to declare poetry "an instrument to transform the world." But the label "social poetry" is appropriate for only a portion of his poems. It is our intention to present an overview of his work, emphasizing its evolution through four distinct periods. Limited space does not allow a thorough analysis of each of Celaya's individual works, but the important tendencies of the four periods are discussed. For the same reason we have concentrated on his most notable stylistic techniques, undoubtedly slighting others which merit analysis. To orient the reader unfamiliar with twentieth-century Spanish poetry, there is an introductory chapter on lyric trends around the time of the Civil War and Celaya's relation to them. The biographical chapter reveals several points of confluence between the poet's personal life and his writings.

Celaya is a prolific writer of some fifty books of poetry, five narratives, six long essays of literary theory and criticism, a drama, and over one hundred thirty articles. To help the reader grasp the essence of Celaya's poetic personality, an attempt is made to discover distinctive themes and features which link his numerous and varied books. A conflict between despair and joy pervades Celaya's work and is also characteristic of his personal life. The stylistic devices which most successfully communicate his intuitions—visionary metaphors, system breakage, dramatic resources, irony, and contrast—depend on conflict for their poetic effect, and conflict also plays an important role in Celaya's personal philosophy of human existence. In the narratives and some dramatic poems, the poet expresses the presence of two kinds of opposing forces in man's nature—feminine forces which lead to a lethargic, sensuous state, and the masculine ones which result in an active, creative life. Celaya is primarily a poet; thus, treatment of his prose is limited to one chapter which emphasizes the relationship of its content to that of the poetry.

I must express my sincere appreciation to Gabriel Celaya for his generous cooperation, graciousness in talking with me on numerous occasions, and attentiveness in answering all my letters. I also extend my thanks to Angel González for his advice, and to those who helped me collect materials: Digna Estévez de Gutiérrez del Olmo, Shirley Mangini González, Juan Ugalde Aguirrebengoa, and María Blasco de Ugalde. Special thanks are due Antonio Ugalde for his encouragement.

SHARON KEEFE UGALDE

Southwest Texas State University

Chronology

1911 Rafael Gabriel Múgica Celaya was born in Hernani, province of Guipúzcoa, Spain, and taken as an infant to live in San Sabastián.

1918 Enrolls in the Marianists' school, *El Colegio del Pilar*, in San Sebastián.

1923–1924 Spends several months with his mother in Pau, France, and in El Escorial, Spain, recuperating from an illness and studying independently. Returns to San Sebastián.

1927 Completes *bachillerato* as an independent student at the public *Instituto*. Begins preuniversity studies. Moves into the intellectually famous *Residencia de Estudiantes* in Madrid. Spends the summer in Tours, France. Both experiences greatly influence his literary formation.

1928 Again travels to Tours for the summer.

1929 Enters College of Industrial Engineering in Madrid.

1934 *Los poemas de Rafael Múgica* (published 1967).

1935 Receives university degree in engineering. Moves from the *Residencia* to San Sebastián where he accepts a position in the family firm Herederos de Ramón Múgica. Spends the summer in England. Publishes his first book, *Marea de silencio* (signed Rafael Múgica); *La soledad cerrada* (published 1947).

1936 Receives the Bécquer Centennial Prize for *La soledad cerrada*. Leaves his position and returns to Madrid to make his living as a writer.

1937 At outbreak of Spanish Civil War, inducted into the Republican army, then taken prisoner and "requisitioned" by Franco's insurgents.

1938 Marriage in San Sebastián.

1939 Returns to his position at Herederos de Ramón Múgica. *Avenidas* (published in *Poesías completas* in 1939).

1940–1944 Disillusioned with literary scene in Spain but continues to write. *Objetos poéticos* (published 1948), *Movimientos elementales* (published 1947), and *El principio sin fin* (published 1949).

1945   Severe depression, ending in physical and mental crisis.

1946   Meets Amparo Gastón who renews his hope and becomes his lifelong companion. *Tentativas*, a narrative.

1947   Founding of Norte Publishing House. *Los poemas de Juan de Leceta* (signed Juan de Leceta) partially published in *Tranquilamente hablando* (1947), and in its entirety in 1961. Translations of Rainer María Rilke *(Cincuenta poemas franceses)*, William Blake *(El libro de Urizen)*, and Jean Arthur Rimbaud *(Una temporada en el infierno)*.

1948–   Period of enthusiasm and prolific literary production, includ-
1954   ing lectures and some sixty articles for newspapers and journals. *Se parece al amor, Las cosas como son, Deriva, Las cartas boca arriba, Lo demás es silencio, Paz y concierto, Vía muerta, Ciento volando* (his first book in collaboration with Amparo Gastón), the narrative *Lázaro calla*, the essay *El arte como lenguaje*, and a translation of Paul Éluard *(Quince poemas)*.

1955   New political awareness and support of Spanish exiles and students' position. *Cantos íberos* and *Coser y cantar* (in collaboration with Amparo Gastón).

1956   Resigns position at Herederos de Ramón Múgica, breaking family ties; moves to Madrid with Amparo Gastón for a full-time literary career. Receives the Critics' Poetry Prize for *De claro en claro*.

1957–   Continues to write untiringly; begins to be recognized
1960   abroad. *Pequeña antología poética* (his first anthology), *Entreacto, Las resistencias del diamante* (published in Mexico and then in a bilingual edition in France), *Cantata en Aleixandre, El corazón en su sitio, Para vosotros dos, Poesía urgente* (published in Argentina), *Música celestial* (last book in collaboration with Amparo), the narrative *Penúltimas tentativas*, and the essay collection *Poesía y verdad*. Some twenty articles also appear.

1961   Spends summer in Acedo in province of Navarra, Spain. *La buena vida, Rapsodia éuskara,* and *L'Espagne en marche* (a bilingual anthology published in France).

1962   Trip to Collioure, France; summer in Acedo. *Poesía (1934–1961)* (an extensive anthology), *Episodios nacionales* (published in France), and *Mazorcas*. His first novel, *Lo uno y lo otro*, also appears marking a period of dedication to prose writing.

1963   Receives the "Librera Stampa" International Prize for his overall poetic production and the Atalya Poetry Group Prize for *Versos de otoño*. *El revelo*, his only drama, and the essay, *Exploración de la poesía*, appear. Increasing fame; begins to be asked for newspaper interviews (some twenty-five published to date).

1964–
1966   Starts spending summers in Miraflores de la Sierra in province of Castile. *Dos cantatas* (includes *El derecho y el revés*), *La linterna sorda*, *Baladas y decires vascos*, and the novel *Los buenos negocios*.

1967   *Lo que faltaba*, *Poesie* (an extensive bilingual anthology published in Italy). Trip to Cuba.

1968   Awarded the Taormina International Prize for *Poesie*. Attends a cultural congress in Havana, Cuba, and visits São Paulo and Rio de Janeiro, Brazil. *Los espejos transparentes*, *Canto en lo mío*.

1969   *Poesías completas*, *Lírica de cámara*.

1970   Judge for the International Prize literary competition in Florence, Italy. *Choix de textes* (an anthology published in France).

1971–
1972   *Operaciones poéticas*, *Cien poemas de un amor* (an anthology of love poems), *Campos semánticos*. New emphasis on literary studies and essays (*Inquisición de la poesía*, *La voz de los niños*, *Bécquer*).

1973   Purchases a small apartment in the old section of San Sebastián and with Amparo Gastón begins to spend several months a year there. *Dirección prohibida; Función de Uno, Equis, Ene*.

1974–
1975   New interest in preparing second editions of his earlier works. Continues to write: *Intinerario poético* (a brief anthology with a long introduction) and *La higa de Arbigorriya*.

1976   Homage to the poet in San Sebastián. Named a member of the "Caballeritos de Azcoita," a group of enlightened Basque intellectuals. *Buenos días, buenas noches*.

1977   Unsuccessful candidate of the Basque Communist Party for a seat in *Las Cortes* (Congress). Continued interest in preparing new editions of earlier works.

CHAPTER 1

The Life and Times of Gabriel Celaya

IN 1936, rebel military forces led by General Francisco Franco, representing the conservative factions of Spanish society, led an uprising against the constitutional government of the recently established Second Spanish Republic. There followed nearly three years of bitter civil war between the right-wing Falangist troops of Franco and the liberal and left-wing defenders of the Republic. The tragedy reached into every region of Spain with the destruction of entire towns and heavy fighting and bombing in the large cities.

When the conflict finally ended in 1939 with the triumph of Franco's forces, over one million Spaniards had lost their lives. The deep ideological division which had caused the strife was irreconcilable, and in order to maintain and strengthen his authority Franco prohibited any freedom of expression. Only the government's position—on all matters—was permitted. The impact of this climate of strict censorship and repression was, of course, felt most directly by the intellectual and artistic communities. Celaya's frank confrontation of the problems of human suffering and the sincerity and forcefulness of his works, appearing when they did, helped keep Spanish poetry from becoming dormant or a mere tool of the regime after the war.

I Poetry in Spain Prior to the Civil War

To understand the historical significance of Celaya's works, the literary trends as well as the political situation should be taken into account. Before the outbreak of the Civil War in Spain, a group known as the Generation of 1927 (Dámaso Alonso, Gerardo Diego, Luis Cernuda, Rafael Alberti, García Lorca, Vicente Aleixandre, Pedro Salinas, Jorge Guillén) formed the poetic mainstream. This

15

group followed the Symbolist tradition, introduced in Spain through
the Modernist tendencies of Ruben Darío, and culminating in the
poetry of Juan Ramón Jiménez. For the Generation of 1927, absolute beauty and formal artistic perfection were of primary importance. Exploration of the subconscious, very personal states of mind
and spirit, and intuitions about the meaning of life were the preferred themes. The poets were less interested in clear communication than in suggesting their unique states of consciousness through
musicality and sensual images. Luis Cernuda has singled out as the
prime characteristic of the early stages of the Generation of 1927 the
cult of the metaphor, which reveals their close relationship with the
poetry of the French Symbolists, Stéphane Mallarmé and Paul Val-
ery.[1] The Generation of 1927 received its name because that was the
year of Luis de Góngora's tricentennial. Influence of Góngora's
style, as well as a general return to classic forms of verse, is typical of
these poets.

By the time the Civil War ended, Spanish poetry had undergone
devastating losses. Miguel de Unamuno, Antonio Machado, and
García Lorca were dead; shortly after, Miguel Hernández died in
prison. The majority of established poets who survived had left
Spain under a self-imposed exile; only three outstanding figures of
the Generation of 1927 continued to live in Spain, Vicente
Aleixandre, Dámaso Alonso, and Gerardo Diego.

II *The Generation of 1936 and the First Postwar Poets*

The poetic mode during the first four or five years immediately
following the Civil War was one of evasion. Undoubtedly the three
years of violent hostility left the spirit of the poets wounded and
weakened. They tried to forget the tragedy, escaping into the soothing realm of music and beauty, following in particular the model of
Garcilaso de la Vega (whose fourth centennial was celebrated in
1936). The tendency to escape reality was possibly also due to fear of
official harassment, as Emilio Alarcos Llorach, one of the best authorities on postwar poetry, suggests in his study of Blas de Otero:
"Neither should the possibility be overlooked of these poets' fear of
being sincere: in order to quiet their inner screams, the most
adequate thing was to distract themselves with minute details and
formal elaborations."[2]

The cult of Garcilaso, formalism, and escapism characterize the Generation of 1936. Most writers of this group had begun to publish shortly before the outbreak of the war, and their interest in classical inspiration and forms continued after the conflict ended. They belong to the same Symbolist tradition as the poets of the Generation of 1927, and manifest great concern for precision and craftsmanship, preferring such forms as the *décima* and the sonnet. The traditional themes of love and landscape descriptions, as well as nostalgic memories of childhood and family life, also are preferred. Luis Rosales, Juan and Leopoldo Panero, Luis Felipe Vivanco, Germán Bleiberg, and Dionisio Ridruejo are outstanding members of the Generation of 1936. The group expanded with the addition of several other poets, including José García Nieto, José Luis Cano, and Enrique Azcoaga. Miguel Hernández and Arturo Serrano-Plaja, although atypical in some respects, are also considered members of this group.

Another important aspect of the early postwar poetry is the presence of religious themes. Some poets maintained the strong faith of their Catholic upbringing, but many others labored to regain or discover the peace that faith brings. The poetry of religious struggle—Leopoldo Panero is an outstanding example—reveals mounting feelings of doubt. The poets confront the reality of their limited temporal existence, reflecting a predominant characteristic of postwar poetry for the first time: "The sense of security is being displaced by a profound feeling of doubt; *poesía arraigada* is losing out to *poesía desarraigada*. As these modifications occur within the religious zone, the sense of abandonment or loss predominates over that of faith and hope. The need of God, the search for Him, and the awareness of His absence are the themes which replace most others. The tone is anguished, confidential."[3]

The tragedy of the Civil War had a very different effect on the first group of postwar poets than it did on the so-called Generation of 1936. Breaking with the Symbolist tradition, this postwar group initiated a new trend: poetry of reality, which boldly deals with the immediate problems of the world and with the eternal problem of man's inevitable death. The fundamental characteristic of Spanish poetry since the Civil War is, according to Vicente Aleixandre, its emphasis on the historical dimension of human life: "It is the song of man, *located*, located in time, time which passes and is irreversible,

and located in space, in a particular society, with some particular
problems which are unique to it and which therefore define it."[4]
The realization of his limited historical existence may lead a poet to
seek inner truths and to try to discover the meaning of his own
individual life, or it may lead him to confront exterior circumstances
as a part of his historical existence. According to how they understood their temporality, the feelings of the postwar poets vacillated
between despair and hope either in their religious faith or in a new
social order. Poetry was no longer art for art's sake, formalism gave
way to a sincere desire to voice the suffering and joys of the community of mankind.

Books by two established and respected poets of the Generation
of 1927 opened the way toward legitimacy for the new realist trend
in Spanish poetry. Especially important in this respect is Dámaso
Alonso's *Hijos de la ira* (Sons of Wrath, 1944), in which the poet
abandons pure aestheticism and concise classic form, often expressing himself in common, everyday language. Emilio Alarcos Llorach
has described the book's effect on Spanish poetry as earthshaking.[5]
The mood of *Hijos de la ira* is one of angry despair which is intensified by the injustice, suffering, and death of the real circumstances
in which the poet was living.

Vicente Aleixandre, probably the most influential poet in Spain at
the time, also manifests new concern for the problems of human
reality in *Historia del corazón* (The Heart's Story, 1954). Over the
years, Aleixandre has been a mentor to postwar poets. He shares
many of their literary views, including the idea that poetry is communication rather than the expression of a unique personal vision,
understandable only by a very select minority. Other poets of the
Generation of 1927 also evolved toward greater concern with human
reality than artistic perfection, but the timely appearance of *Hijos
de la ira* and *Historia del corazón* makes these works especially important.

The first postwar poets began publishing in the late 1940s, principally poets of the *Antología consultada:* Carlos Bousoño, Victoriano
Crémer, Vicente Gaos, José Hierro, Rafael Morales, Eugenio de
Nora, Blas de Otero, Jose María Valverde, and Gabriel Celaya.[6]
Some critics include Celaya among the Generation of 1936 because
he published *Marea del silencio* (Tide of Silence, 1935) before the
outbreak of the Civil War. Celaya published nothing between 1935

and 1946, however, and once he started to publish again, his poetry harmonized with that of the first postwar lyricists, so he is generally considered a member of their group.

Poetry is seen by them as a means of communicating with one's fellowman, of capturing experiences that all men share. A shift from the Symbolists' emphasis on beauty and perfection to an emphasis on content—the human condition—is perhaps the most fundamental change in Spanish poetry in the late 1940s and 1950s. The *Antología consultada* is useful in understanding this change because each author represented summarizes his own ideas about poetry. For example, Celaya exuberantly supports the move away from aestheticism: "Nothing which is human ought to remain outside of our work. . . . A poem is an integration and not the residue which is left when in the name of 'the pure,' 'the eternal,' or 'the beautiful,' a system of exclusion is practiced."[7] Eugenio de Nora similarly warns that formalism often means sacrificing human aspects of poetry.[8] José Hierro concurs that it is the poet's responsibility to deal with the human condition and not escape from existential anguish into some kind of ecstatic contemplation.

These poets express their emotions stridently and frankly. A negative mood of grief and suffering, with the themes of death and fleeting time, predominates in some works, as in Luis Hidalgo's *Los muertos* (The Dead, 1947) and José Hierro's *Tierra sin nosotros* (The Earth Without Us, 1947). In others, the protest against hostile circumstances and inner despair becomes anguished lamentation, *tremendista* in tone, as in the poetry of Victoriano Crémer. The intense confrontation with man's predicament does not always result in hopelessness. A few poets, especially Carlos Bousoño and José María Valverde, produce a religious, meditative response similar to that found in the works of Luis Rosales and Leopoldo Panero. Still other poets find joy in the new promise of the collective existence of mankind.

III   Social Poetry

Many of the poets of the first postwar years focus on the external realities of man's existence. Gabriel Celaya, Eugenio de Nora, Blas de Otero, Leopoldo de Luis, Victoriano Crémer, Ramón de Garcíasol and others advocate and write "social poetry." This new focus was given special force with the publication of the Leonese poetry journal *Espadaña*. Because of his vitality and vocal enthusiasm for his views on poetry, Celaya is the unofficial leader and spokesman for this numerous group of social poets. Initially, he also played an important role in giving momentum to the new realist trend in Spanish poetry. Luis López Anglada considers Celaya and Dámaso Alonso as models for the younger poets who were striving for greater liberty in their poetic expression.[9]

Social poetry—and it should always be kept clearly in mind that this is only one aspect of the new trend toward dealing with the reality of man's limited historical existence—is a move away from *ensimismamiento* ("self-absorption") toward the collective existence of man, from "I" to "we." The suffering and anguish of society —all men, the common masses, the man on the street—become part of the poet's inner feelings. A sense of collectivity and of brotherhood means solidarity in place of solitude, hope instead of despair.

Social poetry also often implies certain ethical values with regard to social issues, such as injustice, freedom, poverty, man's cruelty to man. This facet of social poetry, when moving from the expression of collective feelings regarding certain problems to specific suggestions for solving them, tends to become political, often manifesting support of Marxist doctrine. At the point when the primary goal is to incite men to action, which does happen occasionally, social poetry becomes propaganda and loses its artistic value.[10]

A number of motifs—hunger, suffering of the poor, and the exploitation of workers are related to the ethical values of social poetry. Several motifs are found in the poetry of precursors of the first postwar group. The Peruvian César Vallejo, who together with the Chilean Pablo Neruda influenced Spanish postwar social poetry, frequently uses the hunger motif. The injustice suffered by poor rural people in Spain is a common theme in Miguel Hernández' poetry, and the plight of the workers appears in Serrano-Plaja's *El hombre y el trabajo* (Man and Labor, 1938). These two poets are the outstanding representatives of the Generation of 1936 who, contrary to the dominant Garcilaso trend, did write social poetry.

Social poetry is related to contemporary man's sense of existential responsibility to face the problems of human suffering in the particular circumstances in which he happens to live. The poet feels a moral obligation to deal with injustice. The struggle for a timeless moment of ecstasy, which Juan Ramón Jiménez so longed to achieve, was considered by Hierro irresponsible.[11] In *Antología consultada*, Celaya expresses this ideal: "Poetry is not neutral. No man can be neutral today. And a poet is after all a man."[12]

The language and form of postwar poetry moves away from the formalism and neoclassicism predominating in the Generations of 1927 and 1936. The change is especially evident in social poetry in which the need to reach the masses is a natural outgrowth of the desire to right social injustice. But even in works which focus on the inner dilemma of facing the reality of a limited temporal existence, the poets search for meaning in life by submerging themselves in the suffering and joys of everyday existence. Contact with daily realities, whether in a search for meaning or an attempt to change social conditions, affects the style of the first postwar poets. There is a deliberate move toward simplifying, away from purely decorative complications of syntax, images, and other poetic devices. The most startling change is the profusion with which colloquialisms and everyday words invade the poetic territory.

As a result of the new interest in human and social reality, we also find the narrative aspect of poetry gaining in importance. The poets often describe very specific situations, daily routines, detailed scenes, or even social structures; the need to narrate *(contar)* begins to override the need to sing *(cantar)*. Nearly all the poets of the *Antología consultada* are aware of this change, sometimes described as a return to epic poetry.[13]

IV   The Second Group of Postwar Poets

The second group of postwar poets began publishing in the late 1950s and includes Ángel González, José A. Valente, Caludio Rodríguez, Gil De Biedma, Francisco Brines, Carlos Sahagún, José M. Caballero Bonald, and Eladio Cabañero. With few exceptions, this group pursues the new direction of "poetry of reality." A desire for authenticity makes these poets more open-minded about the possible meaning of life; they sing the simple joys of man's existence as well as the anguish: "Without losing the notion of the temporal and fragile nature of existence, they will feel—even the most elegiaic and satirical—inclined to affirm life, the beauty of the moment in its full consistency."[14] Perhaps the most obvious difference from the previous group is their rejection of the rhetoric and motifs of social poetry which by the late 1950s were often propagandistic and over-used. Solidarity with one's fellowmen, however, remains a fundamental theme.

Although Celaya is appropriately considered a member of the first group, some of his poetry reveals characteristics common to the second: rejection of the rhetoric of social poetry and a sustained hope in the joyous possibilities of life. This affinity with the younger poets is evidence of Celaya's complexity and continual evolution.

V Celaya's Youth and Literary Background

The emotional states expressed by a poet may result from his imagination, but often they proceed from his real life experiences. Therefore, reviewing the poet's life can guide the reader to a clearer understanding of what the poet hoped to communicate. With Celaya, there are important relationships between feelings expressed in his poems and the historic events of his life—for example, his love for Amparo Gastón. Biographical information reveals a poet's literary background—what he liked to read and literary figures he knew personally.

Rafael Gabriel Múgica Celaya was born March 18, 1911, in Hernani in the northern Basque province of Guipúzcoa. He grew up in San Sebastián, home of the Múgica family firm. Gabriel's grandfather was a humble carpenter, but soon the business (which developed during the nineteenth-century industrial boom) brought economic and social success. The firm's overwhelming importance to the family, especially to Gabriel's father Luis Múgica Leceta, proved an obstacle to Gabriel's literary career, a conflict vividly portrayed in the autobiographical novel Los buenos negocios (Good Business, 1965).

In 1918 Celaya began school, attending the private Colegio de El Pilar, run by the Marianist Brothers. For a brief period, 1923–1924, he left San Sebastián because of an illness and spent some time while recuperating in Pau, France, and El Escorial. During these two years he lived a sheltered life, away from other children, even studying on his own without a teacher. His isolation and the overprotectiveness of his mother, Ignacia Celaya Cendoya, affected the twelve year old; it was under these circumstances that Celaya began to write: "I am certain that that regimen was fatal to my mental health. And naturally, it was in that period, when communication was lacking, that I began to write frenetically."[15]

After two years of special treatment, he was considered cured and returned to San Sebastián to complete his *bachillerato* as an independent student. The poet has few pleasant memories of his boyhood; his precocious interest in literature was a constant source of friction with his parents. However, there was one uncle, Enrique Mateo Milano, married to one of his mother's sisters, whom Celaya remembers fondly. He was the only person who encouraged the young writer's literary interests, bringing him recently published books from abroad: "He was the only one who defended me against my parents. Just imagine!—*Against*, because I wrote. A literary career was not taken seriously by them. My obligation was to be an engineer and director of the factory. 'Writing, what a silly business!' my mother used to say."[16] When it was time to consider a university career, the only choice was to study engineering, or go directly to the factory for on-the-job training. Celaya opted for the university because it meant greater freedom to explore his literary interests.

In 1927, after finishing his *bachillerato,* Celaya went to Madrid. He moved into the Residencia de Estudiantes, and together with his cousin Ramón Olhlsson, occupied the room which García Lorca and Salvador Dalí had just vacated. During his stay at the Residencia, eight years in all, the poet was introduced to the world of modern literature. Outstanding literary and intellectual figures of the time visited the Residencia, and on more than one occasion, Celaya was able to chat personally with such figures as Juan Ramón Jiménez, Ortega y Gasset, and Miguel de Unamuno. Celaya also began to read with enthusiasm the works of several members of the Generation of 1927: García Lorca, Moreno Villa, Gerardo Diego, Jorge Guillén, and later, Rafael Alberti, Perdro Salinas, and Vicente Aleixandre.[17] While still living at the Residencia, Celaya met Pablo Neruda and still remembers the excitement among young poets when a Neruda poem appeared in the literary journal *Caballo verde.* Celaya developed a great admiration for the Chilean poet and to this day keeps with pride and affection a poem which he sent to Neruda in 1935 and received back with corrections and comments.[18] Regarding his stay at the Residencia Celaya has said: "It was definitive for my formation."[19]

Celaya's stay in Tours, France, during the summers of 1928 and 1929 also had important consequences for his literary development. He was able to browse in the bookstores and discover for himself the latest Surrealist publications. The owner of the pension where he stayed, Olga Prot de Vieville, showed a special fondness for Celaya and in her enthusiasm wished to guide his literary career, insisting on the importance of French classics, especially Blaise Pascal. Because she had been educated in Germany she also introduced the young poet to "the magic world of the German Romanticists," and Celaya's favorite authors continue to be Johann Goethe and Friedrich Nietzsche.[20]

VI *Engineer or Poet?—A Crisis*

From 1929 to 1935 Celaya studied engineering at the Escuela Central de Ingenieros Industriales. He made routine progress toward his degree, but only halfheartedly; his real vocation seemed to be the arts. He briefly tried his hand at painting, enrolled in humanities courses in the Facultad de Filosofía y Letras, and also did some writing. After graduation in 1935 he began to work for the family company, Herederos de Ramón Múgica, in San Sebastián. That same year his first book of poetry, *Marea del silencio* appeared under the poet's legal name, Rafael Múgica, and his family once again voiced objection to literary endeavor. The Herederos board of directors bluntly stated "that a managing director who wrote verses could prejudice the credibility of the firm."[21] For that reason Celaya's future publications appeared under other names, first Juan de Leceta, and then the definitive Gabriel Celaya.

In 1936, the Bécquer Centennial Poetry Prize was awarded to Celaya for his book *La soledad cerrada* (Enclosed Solitude). This honor encouraged him to leave his position at the factory—he was not genuinely interested in the business and felt uncomfortable—and move to Madrid to attempt to make a living as an author. All plans were disrupted with the outbreak of the Civil War, and Celaya returned to San Sebastián before having settled in Madrid. In March, 1937, he was inducted by the Republican army and was on a short mission in Guernica two weeks before its destruction. When the northern zone was occupied by Franco's forces, he was taken prisoner and "requisitioned" by the other side. Several of Celaya's wartime experiences serve as the basis for portions of *Episodios nacionales* (National Episodes, 1962); the overwhelming confusion and numbing states of horror and grief expressed in this work no doubt reflect emotions experienced personally.[22]

Celaya was married in 1938 in San Sebastián, and when the war ended he returned to his position with Herederos de Ramón Múgica. The period from 1939 to 1946 was a very difficult one for Celaya, culminating in a massive mental and physical crisis. His literary pursuits had been greatly affected by the Civil War. Almost all his respected friends and fellow poets were either dead or in exile, and he was displeased with the escapist trend of contemporary poetry. Celaya continued to write, dedicating himself principally to a narrative entitled *Tentativas* (Attempts, 1946) but because of his disillusionment, he published nothing during the years immediately after the Civil war. In addition, all copies of *Marea del silencio* had been destroyed, and the publication of *La soledad cerrada* by Aguilar disrupted. The frustration of not publishing was only one of the causes of his crisis: "It was really more of a psychological illness. It was my lack of will to live because everything was going so badly. I wasn't publishing, I was desperate in the factory, my family life was a disaster, everything was a disaster. I think the crisis was a type of refuge, an evasion."[23]

Celaya's crisis in 1946 was serious enough to keep him bedridden for six months. During his recuperation, he met Amparo Gastón who was to become his enduring love, strength, and inspiration. Because of her encouragement, Celaya turned with new enthusiasm to literary endeavor, first publishing *Tentativas,* and soon after, other books written during the preceding ten-year period or in the process of completion.

Celaya's optimism following his acquaintance with Amparo contrasts sharply with his previous state of depression. The oscillation between despair and joy is characteristic of his personal life, and of his poetry as well. In a recent interview he described this fluctuation: "You see me now and I am noisy—'How happy! How open!' But I am a man of tremendous lows. However, I am always fighting against them. Looking at this oscillation in perspective, I see it almost as a cycle. I die and am resurrected—I mean, of course, in the sense of depression and the overcoming of it. The process is a completely conscious one. In fact, it is my obsession. I die and am resurrected just as I inhale and exhale, as if it were a type of vital rhythm."[24]

From 1946 to 1956, while still working on Herederos in San Sebastián, Celaya dedicated much of his time to writing. He and Amparo Gastón founded a publishing house called Colección de Poesía 'Norte'; at first Celaya supplied most of the manuscripts, publishing La soledad cerrada, Vuelo perdido (Lost Flight), Movimientos elementales (Elementary Movements) and Tranquilamente hablando (Calmly Speaking). Celaya's translations of Rainer Maria Rilke's Cincuenta poemas franceses, William Blake's El libro de Urizen, and Jean Arthur Rimbaud's Una temporada en el infierno also provided new titles and Norte was able to continue its operation. In their fervor for new literary projects, Gabriel and Amparo even collaborated on writing poetry. Ciento volando (One Hundred Flying, 1953), Coser y cantar (Sewing and Singing, 1955), and Música celestial (Celestial Music, 1958) resulted from their joint efforts.

Norte played an important role in revitalizing poetry after its devastation during the Civil War. The little publishing house contacted the few provincial literary journals in Spain at the time and some Spanish poets in exile. "There was something in the air," Celaya remembers, "and our small publishing house was like a catalyst. It was like returning to 1936 ten years later. . . . We wanted to break the fence of 'official' poetry, and if later we began to turn into one of the first nuclei of social poetry, it was because the development of our poetry demanded it."[25] At first, poets in exile showed little interest or sympathy for the renewed poetic activities of the late 1940s. Celaya recalls that Neruda commented that he did not bother to read poetry then published in Spain because all the poets were Franco supporters. Celaya also remembers León Felipe was the first poet in exile to recognize the effort of those who had stayed in Spain. His support helped gain the interest of foreign poets and other Spanish poets in exile.[26]

Celaya began openly to express his ideas on poetry, writing articles, principally for the daily newspaper of San Sebastián, La voz de España, and giving lectures. By the early 1950s, his political sympathy with the exiles' position and that of the left-wing students was becoming an important force in his life, overtones of which are reflected in *Cantos íberos* (Iberian Songs, 1954). It was at this time that he became very interested in the poetry of Paul Éluard, translating a selection of works under the title *Quince poemas* (1954). His political views, combined with problems at home and a general lack of interest in the family business, led Celaya to decide to leave his engineering job and break his family ties.

VII   *The Writer in Madrid*

In 1956 Celaya moved to Madrid with Amparo, who continues to be an inspiration to him. When Celaya published a collection of love poems called *Cien poemas de un amor* (One Hundred Poems for One Love) in 1971, he dedicated it in the following manner: "To little Amparitxu, who gave me life when I was dead, twenty-five years later."[27] By the time Celaya moved to Madrid he was already well known in poetry circles as a spokesman for new trends. In 1957, his notoriety increased upon being awarded the *Critica de la Poesía* Prize for his book *De claro en claro* (Brightness from Beginning to End, 1957). Celaya's apartment soon became the preferred place for the writers' *tertulias* ("meetings"). There was great interest and debate during the late 1950s and early 1960s about innovations in poetry and the discussions held in Celaya's living room were animated.[28]

Since 1956, Celaya has resided in Madrid, and most of his vacations have been spent in Spain. In the early 1960s he spent several summers in Acedo, Navarra, and in 1964 began to vacation in Miraflores de la Sierra. Since 1973 he has been returning to San Sebastián frequently, staying several months of the year there. As time goes by, he feels ever closer to the Basque people and land where his roots lie.[29] Celaya has made a limited number of trips abroad, principally to France and Italy. Perhaps most significant are his stay in Havana, Cuba in January of 1968 and in the Brazilian cities of São Paulo and Rio de Janiero during the fall of the same year. In both instances he attended writers' conventions.

Celaya has dedicated the last twenty years to writing, producing nearly fifty books of poetry. In addition, he has published some one hundred thirty articles in newspapers and journals, mostly on literary theory and criticism. He has written some long critical essays as well, including *Exploración de la poesía* (Poetic Exploration, 1961) and *Inquisición de la poesía* (Poetic Inquisition, 1972); attempted a drama, *El revelo* (The Revelation, 1963); and, returning to the narrative form of *Tentativas*, published *Penúltimas tentativas* (Next-to-last Attempts, 1960), *Lo uno y lo otro* (One and the Other, 1963), and *Los buenos negocios* (1965).

CHAPTER 2

Surrealist Beginnings:
The First Period, (1934–1944)

W HEN studying a poet who has written as many books as Celaya, it is useful to divide his work into periods in order to perceive its evolution over the years. Special attention needs to be given to the chronology of Celaya's poetry, because confusion about dates could easily arise, especially regarding his first works. Although Celaya published nothing from 1935 to 1946, he was writing during those years.[1] From 1947 on, Celaya has generally published his books as soon as they are finished. Important exceptions are *Los poemas de Juan de Leceta* (Juan de Leceta's Poems) and *Entreacto* (Intermission).[2] A further complication is that occasionally Celaya publishes a work under more than one title.[3] *Poesías completas* (Complete Poems, 1969) is especially useful when considering the evolution of Celaya's poetry because it contains the original groupings and titles of books, which Celaya still considers the authentic ones.[4]

I Celaya Begins to Write

The twelve-year span of the first period extends from the poet's last years at the Residencia de Estudiantes through the year f¹ ꞉ꞏ personal crisis while a director of the family factory, and includes eight books of poetry. In order of composition they are: *Los poemas de Rafael Múgica* (Rafael Mugica's Poems); *Marea del silencio* (Tide of Silence); *La soledad cerrada* (Enclosed Solitude), including "Vuelo perdido" (Lost Flight) as Part II; *La música y la sangre* (Music and Blood); *Avenidas* (Avenues), not appearing in its original form until *Poesías completas* (1969); *Objetos poéticos* (Poetic Ob-

29

jects); *Movimientos elementales* (Elementary Movements); and *El principio sin fin* (Beginning Without End).

When Celaya began writing, he accepted the nature of poetry to be *conocimiento* ("acquisition of knowledge"), a means of exploring the mysteries of life, of discovering his own personal essence, even of creating truth. This concept of the role and significance of poetry is similar to that of Juan Ramón Jiménez and follows a tradition of Symbolist poets. The modern view of poetry as *conocimiento* originated with Charles Baudelaire, who, faced with the breakup of society, turned inward in search of truth and expressed his own rare moments of insight. Jean Arthur Rimbaud, a forerunner of Surrealism, and the Surrealist poets themselves, follow the line of poetry as *conocimiento,* adding their own interpretations. Free from the Symbolists' desire to achieve "pure poetry," the Surrealists attempt to express unusual states of mind in all their complexity, without simplication. During his entire first period, Celaya accepts this Symbolist-Surrealist concept of poetry.

II *Thematic and Emotional Content*

Celaya's ideas about the nature of poetry are closely related to the themes of his early books. Many poems of *La soledad cerrada* exemplify his belief that poetry should explore life's secrets. He delves deep into mysterious realms, seeking to liberate himself from the constraints of a limited human existence. Through his poems he tries to create a perfect instant in which fleeting time and death are annihilated, but the poet can quickly lose hold of the moment of truth. In "Presencia" (Presence, PC 97), for example, he begins the process, referring to his nighttime descent into the depths of silence. In another poem, "Los Presagios" (Omens, PC 100) we find the poet near the secret of death as he senses its presence during the night.

For Celaya the ecstatic moment—if reached—may be a description of nature, the evocation of sexual union, a feeling of oneness with the earth, or simply whatever fills a moment of present time. Some of these experiences are described in *Movimientos elementales* and *Objetos poéticos* and continue to appear in Celaya's poetry periodically through the years. Doreste Ventura emphasizes that Celaya does not reach this state of fulfillment through faith in the supernatural but rather through acceptance of the immediate here and now.[5] The theme of self-limitation is accompanied by sincere feelings of personal joy. Since each instant is significant, everything which fills it—even if previously insignificant, such as a flower or a breeze—is seen with new pleasure, wonder, and reverence. "Pavo real" (Peacock) from *Objetos poéticos* (PC 174) exemplifies the absolute significance of a present moment. This theme is probably an imitation of Juan Ramón Jiménez' last period when he achieved a new awareness of the world during the timeless moment of poetic creation.

Related to the importance of the immediate present is the way in which Celaya reshapes the anguish of his existence into a "poem-thing" made of unique images. "Poema-cosa" (Poem-thing) in *Objetos poéticos* is a vivid example of this process. By seizing his anxieties, the poet diminishes them. Feelings of melancholy, the fearful mystery of death and nothingness are transformed through the creative process into elaborate images in *Los poemas de Rafael Múgica* and *Marea del silencio*.

Often in *Objetos poéticos*, and occasionally in other books of this period, Celaya reaches a state of annihilation of self which leads to a unique pleasure, a feeling of oneness with other human beings and with nature. In "Respirar" (Breathing), for example, the poet expresses a great sense of joy upon experiencing that everything is part of his being, and in "Nocturno" (Nighttime) he loses his individual identity as he becomes united with the night.

Celaya's conquest of joy reflects the influence of Eastern religious philosophies, most notably that of Zen Buddhism. Celaya admits to a lifelong interest in and "a tremendous obsession with Eastern philosophies."[3] *La soledad cerrada* is prefaced by a quote from Upanishad-Bruhadayanka and *Lo demás es silencio*, (The Rest is Silence) by one from Mokahadhrama. In *El derecho y el revés* (The Right Side and the Wrong Side, 1973) Zen is mentioned as a philosophical vogue, and several poems of *Versos de otoño* (Autumnal Verses) reflect a background of Zen thought. Celaya recalls that his early interest in orientalism was not unique; about 1924–1925 Asian thought was gaining importance in Spain. *La revista de Occidente*, influenced by current German trends, published many articles dealing with Eastern philosophies.

Celaya's joyful state of consciousness in *Objetos poéticos*, for example, can be compared with the state of Enlightenment or Nirvana in Buddhism. The poet passes the pessimistic stage of recognition of nonbeing to move on to happiness. Analysis of one's own existence, such as the acknowledgment of man's limitations in "Lo otro" (The Other), and negation of self, as in "Respirar" and "Nocturno," are characteristic of the road to Nirvana. By understanding the nature of our being, we are freed from the anxiety which causes suffering. In *Objetos poéticos*, as in Buddhism, there is no attempt to escape through tranquilizing myths of life after death, of an absolute God, or of a paradise on earth. Another similarity is emphasis on the present moment. [7]

Man's fusion with his elementary beginnings and all of nature predominates in *La música y la sangre*, *Avenidas*, and *El principio sin fin*, appearing occasionally in other books of the period. This union brings peace, because it liberates man from the anguish of a limited existence. The theme, not uncommon in contemporary poetry, is a basic intuition of Vicente Aleixandre, a poet for whom Celaya professes great respect: "There are poets in his group that at certain moments I have admired more, but there is no other who has so consistently and surprisingly held my admiration." [8] During his first period, Aleixandre writes of an elemental world in which animals, vegetables, minerals, and feelings all exist in a cosmic fusion. Man in his natural, primitive state is part of this fusion. However, Aleixandre and Celaya differ in their treatment of this theme. While the latter views the return to primal origins negatively, because it signifies forfeiture of uniquely human attributes in exchange for an escape from anguish, Aleixandre idealizes the primitive, irrational, cosmic fusion into which man enters as a means to achieve the plentitude of a superior life.

Often this theme is formulated in terms of a return to the soil as in "Primavera" (Spring) and "Tierra" (Earth) of *La soledad cerrada*. Soil not only symbolizes man's origins but also his death, reflecting the life cycle. In "El amor y la tierra" (Love and Earth, *La soledad cerrada*), the poet suggests that to enter this irrational realm is to leave behind the anguish that characterizes the human condition; the earth is spoken of as both the cradle and tomb of anxiety. In "Ditirambo" (*El principio sin fin*), the tone is more frenzied; through wild, pulsating, primitive rhythms and sexual hunger one returns to the origins of life.

Celaya most frequently describes the regression to a primitive state in terms of eroticism, especially in *La soledad cerrada*. In other books (*La música y la sangre* and *Avenidas*) he rejects the fusion with nature. The beginnings of life are presented as a paradise lost, as in Aleixandre's works, but the unconscious peace of paradise is discarded in favor of a continuing struggle to understand the mysteries of life: "Misión" (Mission, *Avenidas*).

III *Stylistic Techniques*

Symbolism greatly influenced the young poet's choice of stylistic techniques. The most important characteristics of style during this period are: (1) the use of symbols, reminiscent of the poetry of Juan Ramón Jiménez and the Generation of 1927, and (2) the use of visionary metaphors, visions, and system breakage, reflecting the influence of Surrealism. When Celaya successfully utilizes the expressive possibilities of these techniques, they enable him to convey the intensity and subtle complexity of various emotional states ranging from desperate anxiety to ecstatic joy.

IV *Symbols*

In addition to those symbols which occur only once or twice in Celaya's poetry, there are a few whose consistent reappearance make them worthy of special note. The object represented by the symbol is never material, nor even a clearly identifiable spiritual trait. Rather, the symbol refers to something very vague, pertaining to the emotional realm which can only be spoken of in general terms. In Celaya's poetry the irrationality of the symbol conflicts with our usual, logical way of viewing reality and allows him to communicate at a subconscious, emotional level. For Carlos Bousoño the distinguishing characteristic of a symbol is, "the diffuseness with which we devise the 'real' territory guarded behind it."[9] Because the symbol conveys broad, vague feelings, it is especially appropriate for expressing intuitions about the mysteries of life—one of Celaya's primary concerns during his first period.

Luna ("moon") is one of the most frequently used symbols, especially in *Marea del silencio* and *La soledad cerrada* (for example: PC 53, 65, 83, and 97) This symbol, well within the poetic tradition, is used by Celaya very much as it is by García Lorca, symbolizing the elementary forces of life, sexual passion, and death. The sexual aspect predominates, for example, in "Acebos y luna" (Holly-trees and Moonlight, PC 70) and the death connotation in "No. 37" (PC

71). *Noche* ("night") and *lo nocturno* ("the nocturnal") (PC 82, 139, 142) refer to similar forces. *Alas* ("wings"), *pájaros* ("birds"), *aves* ("wild birds"), and *ángeles* ("angels") (PC 44, 82, 211) symbolize man's capacity for spiritual transcendence. In "Primera inocencia" (First Innocence, PC 135), the poet writes from the pessimistic viewpoint of nothingness, his hopes of transcendence shattered, using the symbol *pájaro*. The vague reality behind *mar* ("sea") and by association behind *marea* ("tide"), *algas* ("seaweed"), *medusas* ("jellyfish"), *submarina* ("submarine"), and *musgo* ("moss"), is the origin of life and death, or sensuality. *Piano* ("piano") (PC 52, 139) symbolizes nostalgic melancholy; *espejo* ("mirror") (PC 68, 90, 139), introspection; and *sonámbulo* ("somnambulist") (PC 56), the poet during the creative process. All these symbols are common to the Symbolist–Surrealist tradition. Celaya's use of colors also reflects well-established symbols: black or *oscuro* ("dark") (PC 49, 100, 103) symbolizes death and suffering; blue (PC 49, 147, 229), joy; yellow (PC 66, 77, 221), aging and death; and white (PC 115, 220, 226), nascent force or sterile loneliness.

Some symbols used by Celaya are infrequent in poetic tradition with the meaning he gives them. *Estatuas* ("statues"), for example, symbolize the relationship of man and time, suggesting the fleeting quality of life, and the silence and nothingness of the mysterious realm of death. When appearing as a symbol, *estatua* is nearly always part of a vision in which it exhibits the impossible phenomenon of slow movement, especially of gestures and eyelids. In poem "36" (*Marea del silencio*, PC 71), the statues half open their heavy eyelids laden with thick grains of salt, and in "23" (PC 57) the poet says that the statues take a thousand years to lower their eyelids and four hundred thousand to open their hands. With the word *virgen* ("virgin"), Celaya alludes to the secrets of human existence and his desperate longing to discover them and transcend his limited historical existence. This symbol is especially effective in *La soledad cerrada*, and often forms the unifying motif of a poem. *Sangre* ("blood") is also used in an original way suggesting the poet's drive to seek answers even though it means suffering and a negation of union with the soothing realm of nature. *Sangre* protests violently against vegetable drowsiness in "Con las fuerzas primeras" (With Pristine Force, *La soledad cerrada*, PC 124).

Perro ("dog") has a special symbolic meaning in Celaya's poetry. In the following example from *Marea del silencio*, *perro* symbolizes the worst in life, all that is base, vile, and repulsive: "Es la hora de las raíces y los perros amarillos" ("It is the hour of the roots and the yellow dogs," PC 77). But already in *La música y la sangre*, Celaya begins to change the symbolic meaning of *perro* to a more positive one, restful contentment (PC 136, 138). Unlike other symbols, the meaning of this one continues to evolve. In later works, *perro* suggests certain very positive qualities in man's nature, perhaps his best and most human ones, his capacity for feelings of love and compassion for others. The first good example of this connotation is found in "Charlot" (Charlie Chaplin, *Entreacto*, 1957). The symbol occurs here as part of a vision: "Hay un perro pequeñito / que te muerde el corazón" ("There is a little tiny dog that bites your heart," PC 566). In *Música de baile* (Dance Music, 1967) and *Lírica de cámara* (Chamber Lyrics, 1969), *perro* alludes to a stubborn defense of all that is human and unique to mankind, not only man's capacity to love but also to think. This symbolic meaning is often extended to *ladrido* ("barking") or *ladrar* ("to bark"). An especially important use of the symbol is found in the concluding sections of *Lírica de cámara* ("Sigma" and "Tau"), in which man's humanness triumphs over a view of him as just another unit of the atomic particles of which the entire universe is made. Although the symbol communicates complex emotional states at a subconscious level, its origin may not be as irrational as it first seems. A dog's faithfulness and inability to change are traits which probably led Celaya to choose it as a symbol of tenacious defense of praiseworthy humanness.

V   *Irrational Metaphorical Techniques*

The most significant influence on Celaya during the early, formative years is that of the Generation of 1927, precisely at a moment when this group was itself being influenced by French Surrealism. André Breton was the original proponent of Surrealism, and he summarized its theoretical premises in a manifesto written in 1924. Surrealism did not originate as a purely literary theory: "It proposed rather to inaugurate an entirely new attitude to life, in which the unconscious mind would guide a man's actions and the reason play a subordinate part. The Surrealist revolution was proclaimed in the name of liberty and under the joint banners of Rimbaud and Marx, as the psychological and economic prophets respectively of the new freedom."[10] In theory this rebellion against logic, highly influenced by the works of Sigmund Freud, meant that a poet should write almost automatically, without thinking, as ideas and images revealed themselves to him during a dreamlike state of semiconsciousness. Celaya is clearly echoing Surrealist theory when he suggests in the poem "Bienaventuranza" (Happiness, *La soledad cerrada*) that the poet who will discover the answers to life's mysteries will be the one who closes his eyes to rational calculations and lets himself be led by irrational dreams.

The year Celaya moved into the Residencia de Estudiantes, 1927, coincides with the time when André Breton's manifesto and the poetry of other French Surrealist writers, especially Paul Éluard, were being introduced in Spain. In several books published shortly afterward by members of the Generation of 1927, the influence of Surrealism in clearly evident: Rafael Alberti's *Sobre los ángeles* (1928), García Lorca's *Poeta en Nueva York* (1929–30), and Vicente Aleixandre's *La destrucción o el amor* (1935). Pablo Neruda's *Residencia en la tierra I* (1935) also reflects similar techniques. The Spanish writers did not adhere to the elaborate theoretical framework which had accompanied Surrealism as it developed in France, but they accepted the importance of the irrational as a rich new source for images and techniques which would enable them to express with greater precision their complex emotions and insights. Like the poets of the Generation of 1927, Celaya borrows from Surrealism those techniques which can increase the expressive capabilities of his poetic language. He is careful to explain that the new metaphors are not simply a decorative, artistic formalism, but rather a daring attempt to capture and communicate the essence of his intuitions.[11]

VI *Traditional versus Irrational Metaphors*

In traditional metaphors there is a rational similarity, usually easily identifiable in the physical world, between the object and the thing with which it is compared. The metaphors found in Celaya's poetry, however, are based on irrational comparisons which are in discord with our normal, logical use of language. But they only appear irrational; the conflict with the normal use of language has a poetic purpose, that of communicating an emotion which ordinary language cannot. In these metaphors, although there is no logical connection between the two items being compared, subconsciously both elicit similar emotions.[12]

Carlos Bousoño distinguishes between different types of irrational metaphorical techniques, each structured in a slightly different way and resulting in somewhat varied poetic effects.[13] As we look more closely at the use of these techniques in Celaya's poetry, a distinction between two types will be helpful. The first group, visionary metaphors *(metáforas visionarias)*, most resemble the structure of traditional metaphors. The second, visions *(visiones)*, are like the images of discordant sensory perception described by Paul Illie which lack an identifiable comparison in the real world.

VII *Visionary Metaphors*

In visionary metaphors, as in traditional ones, an element, *A*, belonging to reality, either spiritual or material, is compared to another element, *B*, either fantastic or real. The difference with respect to more traditional metaphoric expression is that there is no longer a logical connection between the two items compared. The poetic effect takes place at the irrational level with both elements of the comparison eliciting a similar emotional response. During his first period, Celaya makes frequent use of this technique to express the intensity of his feelings and the uniqueness of his intuitions.

We have described the principal theme of *Marea del silencio* as Celaya's confrontation with the agony of existence via poetic creation. In the following strophes from "48" two visionary metaphors help communicate this struggle:

> Vivir como un ángel sufre
> volviendo contra la vida nuestro sueño;
> lo real es una herida de luz que nos duele;
> quisiéramos ser ciegos, ignorarla.
>
> Yo soy un grito vuelto hacia dentro,
> y hacia dentro me estoy muriendo de fiebre;
> para que me veáis solo dejo
> una estatua helada de música y cristal.

To live like an angel suffers, turning our dreams against life; reality is a wound of light that hurts us; we should like to be blind, to be ignorant of it. I am a cry turned inward, and inward I am dying of fever; that you might all see me I leave only a frozen statue of music and crystal. (PC 83)

Both metaphors (lines 3 and 5) are expressed by equating the two elements compared, $A = B$. There is no logical or physical similarity between a wound of light, which itself is fantastic, and our real surroundings. But the emotional likeness is vivid. Opening our eyes to the reality of a limited temporal existence is like a wound of light or truth, because we are forced to feel the pain of nonexistence. The second strophe suggests an attempt to survive the overwhelming anguish through poetic creation. "A cry turned inward" refers to the poet's struggle to examine his innermost being. He feels a desperate need to understand life and capture its mysteries (symbolized by the statue) in poetry.

The joy of a timeless moment, an important theme in *Objetos poéticos*, is frequently expressed through the use of visionary metaphors. In "Horoloquim" (Horology) the pleasures of love limit time to the present moment. The following visionary metaphor—a connecting word now joins the two elements, A *como* ("like") B—conveys the joyous excitement of love: "Tu corazón llevado / como un jardín volante" ("Your heart carried like a flying garden," PC 174). *Corazón* ("heart") is compared to the impossible phenomenon of a flying garden. This unusual and beautiful garden suggests an intense moment of wonder, beauty, and awe, a feeling identified with the heart, which in turn symbolizes the love the girl is capable of giving to the poet.

Celaya also structures visionary metaphors in this way: A, B. The word connecting the real plane with the imaginary one is no longer present. B serves to clarify A and constitutes the poet's second attempt to convey with greater precision the emotion suggested by A. "Se le henchía en el pecho el miedo de una ausencia / una campana blanca con una hormiga dentro" ("The fear of absence swelled in his chest, a white bell with an ant inside," PC 250), from "Acedía" (Acidity) in *El principio sin fin* is a good example of this type. A variation of the theme of union with nature and the beginnings of life, characteristic of this book, is expressed in "Acedía." The poet senses the danger of relinquishing uniquely human qualities in exchange for the numbing tranquillity of union with the unconscious realm of nature. The fear of losing his human spirit is compared with a bell, not a normal bell, but one which has lost its capacity for resounding song. It is incapable of ringing because a minute ant, suggesting irritating frustration, has taken the place of the clangor, and its color, white, suggests sterile loneliness.

VIII   *Visions*

A clash between the logical, normal world and the irrational one also plays an important role in the creation of visions. But there are at least two characteristics which distinguish them from visionary metaphors: (1) The absence of a clearly identifiable real element *A*, and (2) the predominance of the fantastic in what can be considered the equivalent of *B*. Carlos Bousoño gives the following definition: "That sphere of reference (the one referring to reality) does not exist in visions, where I simply see the attribution of fantastic qualities or functions to an object."[14]

Visions combined with symbols account for the most important techniques of Celaya's first two books. The following example from "24" *(Marea del silencio)* illustrates how the poet captures the anguish of imminent death in strange visions:

> Ángeles de aire verde,
> ángeles eléctricos,
> ángeles de cristal y de acero,
> ángeles.
>
> Con sus dedos matálicos y delgados
> entreabrían los párpados
> de las estatuas
> y les miraban absortos y en silencio
> aquellos ojos ciegos,
> inertes,
> vueltos al blanco misterio de lo eterno.

Green air angels, electric angels, angels of crystal and steel, angels. With their thin metallic fingers they would half open the eyelids of the statues, and amazed and in silence those blind, inert eyes, rolled toward the white mystery of the eternal, would look back at them. (PC 58)

The fantastic vision of these angels opening the statues' eyelids is combined with numerous symbols to achieve the poetic effect. The symbolic value of the words used to describe the angels suggests death: green, the color of the rays of the moon, itself a symbol of death; electric, suggesting death by electrocution; glass, a definitive form as is death; and steel, a death-causing material. García Lorca's influence on Celaya during these early years is clearly evident here.[15] The angels convey an eery, fearful feeling of violence and certain death. Not only are they fantastic but they proceed to undertake the rationally impossible by opening the statues' eyelids. Blind, inert eyes and the white mystery—symbol of sterile loneliness and death—suggest a sense of horror. The poet has transformed his agonizing obsession with death into vivid images which allow him to communicate the intensity of his feelings.

Through visions Celaya expresses a wide gamut of emotions and those found in "Pavo real" (Peacock) in *Objetos poéticos* contrast with the anguish discussed above. The joyful elation of limiting oneself to the present moment is the theme of "Pavo real," from which the following strophes have been taken:

> Explosiones lentas
> del manzano en blanco;
> las rosas, volcanes
> ardiendo despacio.
>
> Poco a poco se abre
> el esplendor lejano
> y un silencio transciende
> del aire y del árbol.

Slow explosions of apple trees in white: volcanos slowly burning. Little by little distant splendor opens, and from the air and trees a silence transcends. (PC 174)

The vision of an apple tree slowly exploding into whiteness has some relationship to the real world, a blossoming tree. But the poet expresses himself in visionary terms because he is not describing an orchard scene but his own interior landscape, his explosive joy with the discovery of living only in the present. He is at last free from anxiety and his immediate surroundings acquire a paramount importance. The vision is followed by a visionary metaphor which compares roses with slow-burning volcanos. Again, rationally, there is little similarity, but at the emotional level the roses of a given present moment are as marvelously overwhelming as the sight of an active volcano. The vision and visionary metaphor are mutually supportive because the concept of explosion has a role in each of them.

Man's enduring sexual drive is the theme of "Un Antiguo deseo" (Ancient dream) in *El principio sin fin.* A logically possible scene opens the poem, a girl standing near a river, surrounded by the animal inhabitants of the area. Abruptly the following fantastic visions appear: "dientes de otro tiempo" ("teeth of another age"), "ojos que se hacen del tamaño de un iris" ("eyes that become rainbow-size"), and "uñas que erizan edades congeladas" ("fingernails which make ice ages bristle up," PC 237). The poet knows that sexual hunger (teeth) is as ancient as mankind (other ages, ice age), and the force of this enduring desire is conveyed by eyes that grow inconceivably large when contemplating the naked girl. Finally, the violent side of the sexual drive is suggested by the vision of the fingernails.

IX *System Breakage*

The liberating force of Surrealism opened the way for the development of another poetic technique based on a rupture of our normal perception of life. A clash between a logical view of reality and a disruptive, irrational perspective is the core element of this device. It is not a recent innovation, but the illogical component of this technique made it appealing to those twentieth-century writers who had been influenced by the expressive possibilities of the irrational. System breakage dates back at least as far as the Spanish Golden Age, and was used extensively by Francisco de Quevedo. Only since its return to vogue, however, has system breakage been analyzed by literary critics, most notably by Carlos Bousoño. The following definition is crucial in understanding how this device works: " 'System' signifies here 'norm' (an instinctive norm or one based on experience or even convention), firmly rooted among *most men.*"[16] When one element of a system appears, A, there is a natural expectation that it will be followed by another member of the same system, B. What the poet does is to break the system A–B, following A with some other element, X, not normally part of the suggested system. X is not arbitrarily selected, but chosen with the aim of achieving a specific poetic effect.

The usual elements of a system (some mentioned and others inferred) modify the meaning of the object which breaks the system. In this way the disruptive element, in conflict with the previously harmonious system, becomes a synthesis of its own meaning plus the meaning and connotations of the regular members of the system. Underneath the apparently irrational combination is the poetic rationale that each member of the series communicates some aspect of the poet's emotional state; taken together, they enable him to convey his intuition without sacrificing its complexity. This same technique was termed "chaotic enumerations" by Leo Spitzer, and it is found frequently in the poetry of Vicente Aleixandre and Pablo Neruda.[17]

During the first period and especially after the third book, *La música y la sangre*, Celaya repeatedly uses system breakage as a means of transforming everyday language into poetic language. The juxtaposition of adjectives from two different fields of reference (or systems) helps the poet to express his intuitions about the essence of eroticism in the following verse of "La sulamita" from *Avenidas:* "tu piel morena y lenta" ("Your brown, slow skin," PC 158). Here the technique serves to express the synthetic complexity of the intuition. *Morena* belongs to a field which describes the inanimate, material quality of color. This term is appropriate for a description of the skin, and visually suggests the real presence of a specific girl. *Lenta* is a member of another system, something capable of independent movement, and is not normally used to describe human skin. The connotations of *piel lenta* are related to the previous line, "Aunque tan solo sea tu lisa piel de sierpe" ("even though it is only your smooth serpent's skin"), and suggest the primitive, serpentlike movements of the woman. By combining these two words as if they belonged to the same system, the poet succeeds in conveying his complex feelings about his beloved. For him, she is both a real person and a means of escape into the irrational realm of the elemental world.

"Como un ave" (Like a Bird, PC 219) in *Movimientos elementales* is almost entirely made up of series of broken systems. The irrational enumeration enables the poet to express a beautiful moment of peace. Freedom from anxiety allows him to experience life with new intensity and to discover joy in what previously seemed to be insignificant events. Although not logically related to each other, items in the series suggest the same idea: an increased capacity for perception. Sight is emphasized as the poet perceives a "small bit of palpating shadow," an "apple against the ardent whiteness of summer," a "great heart in the air," "closed islands in a remote pause of the clearest seas," soft light, and a ship careening on round waves. The hush suggested by the various members of the series, "a delicate deer," "a long breeze," "some unspoken words," silence, peace, and "a caress in the elongated form of a bird," emphasize the poet's keen sense of hearing. The enumerated items also enable the poet to express the belief that he has reached a new state of truth and joy by living each moment to its fullest. This is achieved through the symbolic value of the whiteness, clarity, and light found in the series.

There is a special type of system breakage, breakage of logical systems, also called paradox, in which opposites are stated as being equivalent. Our logic tells us that black is different from white and that black does not equal white. 'Black is white' would be an example of logical system breakage. Bousoño mentions two important factors to remember regarding this variation. First, that in making two opposing terms equivalent, one must be used metaphorically so that it only appears to contradict the other term, but does not, in fact, do so. Secondly, paradox is used to reinforce other techniques, never alone. The following verse of "Mar mecido" (Agitated Sea) in *El principio sin fin* embodies both these points: "una piel irisada que, cambiando no cambia" ("a rainbow-hued skin which changing does not change," PC 242). *Cambiando* really modifies *no cambia*. The poet is referring to an elemental truth of life which never changes, the force of sensuality, even though individuals enacting it may vary. The paradox occurs here in conjunction with two other important techniques, system breakage and a visionary metaphor. The last line of the same stanza contains another example of paradox: "música lenta, tan lenta que no suena" ("Slow music, so slow that it is not heard," PC 242). This silent music suggests the hypnotic, pervasive force of sensuality.

X   Combined Use of Techniques

The principal poetic techniques of the first period, symbols, visionary metaphors, visions, and system breakage, are generally somehow combined. The poetic effect is often further enhanced by other minor or less frequent devices. "Vida nueva" (New Life) in *La*

música y la sangre, manifests the careful interweaving of four different techniques:

> Los sueños derribados,
> como toros enormes, como nubes,
> como ángeles con garras y alas turbias
> revueltas por la música y la noche,
> se mueven entre espasmos todavía.

Demolished dreams, like enormous bulls, like clouds, like angels with claws
and muddy wings, stirred by the music and the night, still shake among
spasms. (PC 145)

The metaphorical and system-breakage techniques of this stanza are
composed of a central vision which is modified by a series of visionary metaphors. In addition, the last member of the series includes a
break in the system of attributes normally associated with an object
and a symbol. "Demolished dreams . . . still shake among spasms"
is the central vision. "Like enormous bulls," "like clouds" and "like
angels . . . night," make up the series of visionary metaphors
modifying the emotional significance of "demolished dreams." The
break in a system of attributes appears as part of the last member of
the visionary metaphor series, when the angel's hands are described
as "claws." The symbol *noche* ("night") is also part of the last
member of the series. The poetic intuition expressed in this stanza is
complex. Love becomes so central in the life of the poet that he is
spiritually reborn. He expresses this feeling by suggesting a rejection of all former illusions, even those to which he has clung in
hopes of a more perfect existence, and which were basic to his entire
life.

"Rapto" (Rapture) in *La soledad cerrada,* has been selected as a
final example because it reflects many of the outstanding characteristics of Celaya's initial poetry. The poet himself has indicated
that *La soledad cerrada* is the most representative book of the first
period and included "Rapto" in his recent anthology, *Itinerario
poético* (Poetic Itinerary, 1975), which contains very few early
poems.[18] The Surrealist idea that creative ability reaches its peak
during the night hours of vigil when the poet is on the threshold of
the subconscious dream world is the theme of "Rapto."

Virgen ("virgin") symbolizes the mysteries of death and a desperate longing to understand them. This symbol is the principal poetic

device of "Rapto," repeated throughout the poem, embodying the theme and unifying the nineteen strophes. The desire to seize the *virgen* is presented in terms of sexual passion, similar to the symbolic use of the union of lovers by San Juan de la Cruz (St. John of the Cross). Celaya acknowledges the influence of the sixteenth-century poet and introduces the poem with a quote from one of San Juan's works. Other symbols all relating to the mysterious realm of death *luna* ("moon"), *noche* ("night"), *oscura* ("dark"), and *estatuas* ("statues"), enhance the poem's expressiveness.

Celaya is able to communicate the intensity of his anxiety about death by combining these symbols with other prominent techniques of the first period. "El cielo es un círculo de gritos detenidos / que ilumina la súbita luz del espanto," ("The sky is a circle of trapped screams which illuminates the sudden light of horror," PC 93) and "El cielo es el vacío de un éxtasis redondo / girando alrededor de un culminante asombro" ("The sky is the emptiness of a circular ecstacy spinning around a supreme terror," PC 93), are two parallel visionary metaphors of the type $A = B$ which increase the poet's success in expressing his terrifying anguish. The accumulation of the connotations of words like "shout," "sudden," "fear," "emptiness," and "astonishment" all relate on the emotional level to the poet's horror in the face of death.

The formation of a visionary metaphor through the use of system breakage makes its significance felt more intensely by the reader. "Plantas de carne" ("flesh plants"), a fantastic image which breaks the system of normal types of plants, is equated with "hombres dormidos" ("sleeping men"). A struggle against the danger of becoming an insensitive, nonthinking being is the poet's destiny. The interweaving of techniques allows Celaya to express this complex intuition.

Much of what Celaya learned and wrote during his early years as a poet never left him. For example, the irrational metaphorical tehniques continued to be used, especially in the second and fourth periods. Likewise, techniques which later gained importance are often found sparingly and timidly rehearsed during the first period. But we can point to symbols, visionary metaphors, visions, and system breakage as characteristic of the first period because during these years they are Celaya's *principal* means of achieving poetic effect. Later, these techniques are combined with other more important ones.

Neither does the close of the first period signify Celaya's definitive abandonment of the concept of poetry as *conocimiento*. Such themes as union with nature and the perfect present moment also reappear. But the most formidable link between the first period and those which follow is Celaya's fluctuation between states of anguish and joy. The books written between 1934 and 1944 clearly reveal the interrelationship between these two contrasting emotional states. The joy expressed—a timeless moment, annihilation of self, a return to the elementary beginnings of life, eroticism—is a manifestation of the poet's struggle to overcome the agony of the human predicament.

CHAPTER 3

A Poetic Confrontation
with Existential Anguish:
The Second Period, (1945–1954)

DURING the second period Celaya achieves a unique form of
poetic expression. He conveys his feelings—a newfound love,
faith in the communion of mankind, and continued anguish—with
great intensity by combining what was learned during his formative
years with new poetic resources. The result is some of Celaya's best
and most characteristic poetry.

The changes of the second period are clearly exemplified in the
books, *Avisos de Juan de Leceta* (Juan de Leceta's Warnings) and
Tranquilamente hablando (Calmly Speaking) known together as *Los
poemas de Juan de Leceta* (Juan de Leceta's Poems). The emotions
expressed seem much more intense and real than those manifested
in previous works, because they are conveyed in language closer to
our everyday existence. Familiar words and expressions abound; the
poet's feelings of pain and anguish are communicated with tremendous impact, as if they were part of our own daily lives. *Los poemas
de Juan de Leceta* are of special significance in Celaya's poetic production. The familiar, direct tone and the realities of the *más acá*
("here and now"), introduced as themes here, are important in
nearly all of the rest of his poetry. The force of their directness are
characteristic of Celaya's subsequent social poetry, and the clarity
and intensity of their simple immediateness, of later books. And
whether expressing despair, joy, or faith in human solidarity, Celaya
has continued to write of these themes as experienced in the concrete circumstances of the real world.

47

I *Thematic and Emotional Content*

An overview of the eight books of poetry written during the second period closely reflects important personal and ideological changes the poet underwent during those years. For Celaya, 1946 was a year of mental and physical crisis; at times he was so desperate as to consider suicide. This despair is communicated in the two initial books of the period, *Avisos de Juan de Leceta* and *Tranquilamente hablando*, both written during 1945 and 1946.

The mood of these books resembles that of the twentieth-century French Existentialists. It was just after World War II that Existentialism was having its greatest impact in Spain, although the trend had been introduced much earlier. Prior to the Spanish Civil War, literary magazines such as *Cruz y Raya* had published pieces by Martin Heidegger. Later, when the movement gained strength in Spain, it was not Heidegger but the French Existentialists Albert Camus and Jean-Paul Sartre who served as models. Celaya realizes that this influence came at a crucial time in his life, when he was undergoing a process of crisis and change.[1]

The theme of anguish predominates in *Avisos de Juan de Leceta*, usually expressed in terms of cynicism rather than physical nausea. Celaya's premise here is that life is meaningless and empty. We can fill this nothingness with certain routines and activities, but all are mere disguises of inevitable death. "La vida que uno lleva" (The Life that One Endures) and "Cosas que pasan" (Things that Happen) are good examples. At times love and other joyous trivialities can fulfill us and we forget our condition. In a few poems at the end of the book, "La primavera se estrena" (The Premiere of Spring) and "Camino de Zumaya" (On the Road to Zumaya), for example, feelings of joy are expressed. There is a foreshadowing of Celaya's future espousal of social poetry in "A vuestro servicio" (At Your Service). The poet's loneliness will eventually lead him to declare himself the spokesman of the humble masses. There are as yet no strident proclamations of human solidarity, only the intuition that isolation intensifies anguish.

Resignation in the face of life's meaninglessness is the principal theme of *Tranquilamente hablando*. Even though the poet views the human condition with greater calm, he still is not at peace. In "Tranquilamente hablando" (Calmly Speaking) and "Este mundo nuestro" (This World of Ours), he finds himself surrounded by a noisy, rapid, hostile world, and his resignation results in greater solitude rather than joy. Man destroys the possibility of simple life in harmony with nature by inventing the stockmarket, political parties, and wars, as expressed, for example, in "Todos las mañanas cuando leo el periódico" (Every Morning When I Read the Newspaper). The poet presents himself as a poor, sensitive soul, helpless in the face of an anonymous, indifferent world. However, there are moments of relief; the feeling of being at one with other men—all must live through the same problems—brings a certain sense of tranquillity, as expressed in "Mi cuarto con el balcón abierto" (My Room with the Balcony Wide Open). If happiness is found it is because of silly, little, everyday pleasures, like looking at pink corsets in a display window, "Escaparate-Sorpresa" (Window Surprise). At times the poet is happy with things as they are, implying a similar acceptance of the here and now as found in *Objetos poéticos*. But Celaya never expresses profound inner joy in this book, because as soon as he feels alive and happy, the thought of death returns. During the middle years of the second period Celaya finds alternatives to anguish but the final book, *Entreacto* (Intermission), is an abrupt return to the expression of despair, now hidden behind an ironic facade of clownlike capers. This reappearance of despair underlines the essential characteristic of Celaya's poetry: the fluctuation between despair and joy.

In a chance encounter in a bookstore in 1947, Celaya met Amparo Gastón, and to this day he believes that she saved him from his severe crisis and led him back to a productive literary career.[2] *Se parece al amor* (It Resembles Love), the third book of this period and the first after meeting Amparo, is a sudden burst of life and joy, contrasting sharply with the two previous books. Love, passion, and fascination with the beloved, who is always near yet always evasive, are the predominant themes. In many poems, Celaya successfully conveys a feeling of growing desire in the presence of the loved one. The passion expressed here is a universal one, lacking the personal tenderness expressed in some later love poems.

Celaya's love for Amparo was like a catalyst. Suddenly he was alive, experiencing life with new eyes, and striving to understand his relationship to the world around him. One reaction, reflected in *Las cosas como son* (Things As They Are), is the determination to accept the here and now and enjoy all the pleasures life has to offer. The anecdotal situation presented is the poet paying his last respects to a dead friend, Pablo. It is a long poem (eighty-six *décimas*) in the form of a dramatic monologue and summarizes three attitudes toward life: First, anguish: What is human life? Why do we die? Second, resignation and acceptance of death as part of life. Third, the great joy which results from such an acceptance. Many alternatives to anguish are suggested, such as sex and the creation of civilization, but none is sufficiently powerful to annihilate death. In a climactic moment in the poem, the poet views life as a choice between suicide and the acceptance of death. Presented in these terms, he suddenly perceives with clarity that by living only in the present moment the anguish of nonexistence after death vanishes. The poem closes with the triumphant statement "Pablo has died, but I am still living" (PC 348).

The historical circumstances—the devastating effect of the Spanish Civil War and the continued suffering and atrocities in Europe with the advent of World War II—had an impact on poetry. Like many other poets, Celaya began to reexamine his works. Their individualistic, irrational metaphorical techniques and very personal insights seemed somehow irrelevant in face of the immediate problems of everyday existence. Celaya felt a new necessity to express the suffering of the masses and a united hope for the future. The focus of Celaya's poetry moves from the expression of individual emotions to those which stem from the collective experience.

The appearance of the themes of brotherhood and social injustice in Celaya's poetry are in part a reaction to the suffering and oppression which he witnessed during the Civil War and the postwar years. They are also, however, literary imitations of the works of other poets who, some ten years earlier, had expressed similar feelings of solidarity with those who suffer from social injustice— Miguel Hernández, Rafael Alberti, Arturo Serrano-Plaja, and Pablo Neruda.

Close to the end of the third period, in *Paz y concierto* (Peace and Concert), Celaya embraces the collective spirit of mankind. In clear, strong words he supports the belief that the poet must sing of "we"—not "I"—and with this change comes new hope and joy through communion. In an introduction entitled "Nadie es nadie" (Nobody is Anybody), Celaya describes the new direction of his poetry: "Let's not reach out toward others to talk to them about our own peculiarities. Let's abandon the miserable temptation of trying to make our introspective self last for ever. Let's be like those poets—the great ones, the unique ones, the universal ones—who, instead of speaking to us from outside, as in confession, speak from within us and for us, as if they were we, and cause that identification of us with them and them with us which gives authenticity" (PC 501–2). The poet now presents himself without a *yo* ("ego") and without his obsessive preoccupation with death. The emptiness remaining is filled with the life and feelings of the rest of humanity, especially of the humble masses who labor incessantly without transcendental preoccupations, as expressed for example in "El martillo" ("The Hammer").

Celaya's new mission, singing of the collective hopes and suffering of mankind, struggles against his previously held belief that poetry is meant to express the deep personal intuitions of the poet's innermost being. In *Las cartas boca arriba* (Showing One's Cards), in a frank, epistolary style, as if addressing an intimate friend, both views of life are expressed. Each poem is written to a particular person, among them several poets, Pablo Neruda, Blas de Otero, Miguel de Labordeta; a painter, Jesús de Olasagasti; and there is also one written to Celaya's double, Juan de Leceta. The tone of the book vacillates between joy and despair, with a positive attitude predominating. Only one poem, "A Carlos Edmundo de Ory," ends on a pessimistic note. Often anxiety is portrayed as the emotional characteristic of the person to whom the poem is dedicated. The poet tries to convince his friends that life is not only despair but can be a marvelously happy experience. In "A Blas de Otero" Celaya attempts to inspire hope by renewing his friend's faith in the significance of poetry, and in "A Andrés Bastrera" Celaya tries to convince this worker that a new communion among men can be his salvation. There is a special note of enthusiastic joy in the poem dedicated to Pablo Neruda because Celaya greatly admires Neruda's newfound faith in the collective existence of mankind.[3] In describing the tension between joy and despair in his friends, Celaya is at the same time painting a self-portrait.

Lo demás es silencio (The Rest is Silence) embodies the poet's inner struggle to choose between "private" (introspective) poetry and "public" (collective) poetry. The struggle is presented in terms of a dramatic conflict between three characters. The *Protagonista* ("Protagonist") continually tries to understand his identity and his destiny. He is tormented by the thought that his individuality ends with death and never succeeds in finding an answer which can

appease his anguish. *El Coro* ("The Chorus") represents the suffering masses, preoccupied with hunger and disease, not the ultimate
meaning of life. According to Celaya, *El Mensajero* ("The Messenger") represents a rigid, Marxist position which clashes with the
Existential Protagonist.[4] The Messenger brings good news, assuring the chorus that man's only hope is to work together here on
earth, indifferent to the Protagonist's dilemma. The Chorus immediately accepts the message, but the Protagonist is unable to
place his faith in the new cause. Finally, he resigns himself to silence out of respect for those who still have hope. In this poem
Celaya has still not totally rejected his former views in favor of social
poetry.

II *Stylistic Techniques*

The stylistic changes of the second period reflect Celaya's new
sensitivity to external realities and the need to communicate with
his fellowman. There is a new directness and intensity to Celaya's
poetry, achieved in part through the use of everyday language and a
conversational tone. There are literary precedents; the intensity of
the anguish, the lack of ornamentation, and the starkness of expression are reminiscent of the poetry of Miguel de Unamuno and Antonio Machado. More significant still is the influence of Miguel
Hernández, whose use of rustic, everyday terms, as well as ener-
getic forcefulness, achieved through such devices as repetition and
parallelism, is reflected in Celaya's poetry.

One of the most significant changes in Celaya's poetry during
these years is his new use of irony, perhaps the most successful
poetic technique during this period and again in the fourth. It may
be an imitation of Antonio Machado's irony in his later works such as
"Siesta. En memoria de Abel Martín" *(Canciones a Guiomar y
varios lamentos*, 1936).[5] Irony is found also in some poetry of the
second period of the Generation of 1927: "A new age of Spanish
poetry has begun: the age of the cry, of vaticination, of hallucina-
tion, or of gloomy irony," and perhaps Celaya was made aware of its
effectiveness by them.[6] Celaya's use of irony, however, seems to be
more an imitation of that found in León Felipe's first books. For example, the poetic speaker of "No hay dios" *(Español del éxodo y del
llanto*, 1939) is made to appear nonchalant, speaking in a casual,
conversational tone, and often in direct dialogue. This type of irony
is found frequently in Celaya's works.

In spite of the changes evident in Celaya's second period of poetic production, he does not reject altogether the techniques of the first period. System breakage remains important and appears with new variations, including breakage of systems of social convention, of attributes, linguistic patterns, and experience. Irrational metaphorical techniques, although employed much less frequently, continue to be used by Celaya, especially when he wishes to contrast an introspective, individualistic understanding of life and poetry with one which highly esteems a collective spirit among men.

One of the ways Celaya creates his new tone of urgency, forcefulness, and directness is through the use of colloquialisms and a conversational tone. How can everyday language create a poetic effect? Celaya answers that poetic language achieves its effect by taking us unaware, not because it is highbrow. It catches us by surprise and thus fixes our attention on what is being said.[7] Referring specifically to a book of his second period, Celaya explains how everyday language forms the surprise necessary for a poetic effect: "To begin with, if plain language—or prosaic expression, as my adversaries called it—attracted me, it was not only the desire to facilitate communication with the reader unwilling to make an effort, but rather because after Surrealism and Garcilasismo it sounded extremely refreshing, and by what is only an apparent paradox, plain language gave me the poetic shock and indispensable surprise that I could no longer find in any metaphor, no matter how daring or how knowledgeable it might have been."[8] As will be shown, this conversational tone is a basic element of Celaya's use of irony, and is especially important in *Los poemas de Juan de Leceta, Las cosas como son*, and *Entreacto*. In other works of this period Celaya combines his "surprising" tone and language with visionary metaphorical techniques and system breakage. This synthesis predominates in *Las cartas boca arriba* and is also frequent in *Paz y concierto*.

Many elements form Celaya's casual tone, beginning with avoidance of a highly refined vocabulary. Common, everyday words are the principal source from which Celaya selects his poetic vocabulary, often including words not previously considered acceptable in poetry. Even more important in the creation of the new directness is the use of colloquial expressions such as "¡qué pena!" ("What a shame!"), "porque sí" ("Just because"), and "no es poca cosa" ("It's quite something"). Avoidance of embellishment makes the use of everyday language even bolder. The use of the first person, presented as a conversation with only one person speaking (extended to actual dialogues in the long dramatic poems) or as a letter to a friend, helps contribute to the informal stance. Questions, parenthetical asides, direct address, and commands are also important.

Celaya at times begins a poem abruptly, without background information, as if the reader had suddenly begun to overhear someone's conversation. "A Jesús Olasagasti" (*Las cartas boca arriba*) begins in the following abrupt manner: "Es tremendo, Jesús: no nos dejan ser niños" ("Its just terrible, Jesús, they won't let us be children," PC361). Immediately the reader becomes a privileged observer in a candid exchange between friends, and the poem's impact increases as the reader accepts what is being expressed as sincere and confessional. The same poem, in addition to colloquialisms and direct address, contains another element of the conversational tone: anecdotal presentation.[9] The friends meet, reminisce, chat, and give each other advice. When they part company at the end of the poem, the poet gives his friend a final word of encouragement as he says good-by: "May the angel of Ibaeta take you by the hand!" (PC 364).

III *Forms of Irony*

Some of Celaya's most powerful poems communicate intensity of feelings through the combined use of familiar, direct language and irony. Irony characteristically appears when the poet wishes to express a grim, desperate reaction to life's meaninglessness. With the collapse of all established beliefs, this use of irony has become a frequent component of modern literature and is perhaps Celaya's most successful means of expression. In his work, irony suggests another source of unity between form and content. Conflict not only accounts for the fundamental emotional state, despair–joy, but it is also a basic component of irony. In irony there is a clash of emotions, something is felt to be both funny and painful, both comic and Tragic. A. R. Thompson has defined its essential feature as "discrepancy or incongruity between expression and meaning, appearance and reality, or expectation and event."[10] Irony is capable of causing a powerful emotional reaction in the reader, first, because two conflicting emotions appear juxtaposed, and second, the final, overall response is delayed. Through intellectual participation the reader discovers the pain behind the wry smile, and this discovery makes him feel at one with the author and psychologically set to participate in the underlying emotion. According to what Celaya is attempting to communicate, irony can produce a kindly, compassionate reaction or a grimly bitter effect.

To facilitate analysis of irony in Celaya's poetry, it will be useful to consider four different types. There is some discrepancy among critics as to just what the component parts of irony are, but the four types described here are generally accepted, although sometimes with different labels. Verbal irony is the basic type, the easiest to submit to stylistic analysis: "The implication of what is said is in painfully comic contrast to its literal meaning. This irony ranges from crude sarcasm to profound philosophical observation or tragic utterance."[11] Two devices are commonly used to achieve the discord between the literal meaning of what is said and how it is said. Inversion, saying the opposite of what is meant, has often been used to convert apparent praise into reproach or, conversely, reproach into praise. The other device, understatement (litotes in the terminology of rhetoric), is found much more frequently in Celaya's poetry. As David Worcester points out, inversion, as well as litotes, is really a type of understatement: "Even where a sentence must be reversed, not exaggerated, a striking observation is concealed under an unemotional, matter-of-fact surface."[12]

A matter-of-fact surface may also be part of irony of manner in which a "person's true character is shown to be in painfully comic contrast to his appearance or manner."[13] A character may appear plain, with no particular philosophy or ideals, somewhat naive and simple, when in fact he is expressing a complex criticism of society and the anguish of alienation. Irony of manner may relate to the author when he assumes a deliberate pose, as does Chaucer in *Canterbury Tales,* or to manipulation of a literary personality, as in the case of the hero of satires such as *Gulliver's Travels.*

The third type, irony of events, also called dramatic irony, results from the painfully comic incongruity of how events appear to be taking shape and their final outcome. The events themselves, chosen by the author, contain the irony which must be discovered by the reader without the warning signals of verbal irony or the author's deliberately assumed mood. In drama containing irony of events, many individual speeches may give an ironic effect. But as Thompson is careful to point out, "their irony derives from the event, not from themselves, and they are innocent of irony if they stand alone."[14]

Cosmic irony is the fourth type. Worcester selects this label to describe a relatively new development in the use of irony which is frequently found in nineteenth- and twentieth-century literature. His discussion of this phenomenon clarifies its characteristics and explains why the term "cosmic" was chosen. The Copernican revolution, in contrast with the Ptolemaic system, revealed man's total insignificance in the cosmic system. The blow of the discovery was initially buffered by religious beliefs, but gradually over the centuries its full effect has come to be felt. The result, explains Worcester, is as follows: "The expansion of the cosmos allowed the ironist to place his judgment seat at a point so infinitely remote from human affairs that every 'law' of sentiment, faith, and morality lost its absolute sanction and appeared as strictly human makeshift."[15] Tedium, the revolt against God, and the earth as a speck of dust are mentioned as themes of cosmic irony. Cosmic irony is essentially the same as the "ironic vision" that Charles Glicksberg finds so prevalent in modern literature.[16] Man, stripped of his significance in the universe, with his actions of no value, without absolutes to sustain him, laughs tragically at his destiny.

These separate categories are only an artificial means of helping to clarify our analysis; actually, in Celaya's poetry, these types are very frequently used together. Most commonly, Celaya combines cosmic irony with one of the others. There are instances of complex combinations of all the variations. Irony of manner is the type most effectively used by itself. During the second period, irony is used consistently and very successfully in the following books: *Los poemas de Juan de Leceta* and *Entreacto*. It also appears to a lesser extent in *Las cartas boca arriba*.

Los poemas de Juan de Leceta, especially the first section, "Avisos" (Warnings), offers many excellent examples of this effective combination. In "Vacaciones caras" Expensive Vacations) and "¿Y qué?" (So What?), tedium is the theme of cosmic irony. In the former, Celaya intimates that the normally fun-filled vacation time is really no more than another empty routine, incapable of alleviating loneliness and anguish. In retrospect, the use of ironic understatement in the title suggests the total emptiness of man's life. The vacation is expensive in terms of something much more significant than the money the title implies, for it confirms the poet's spiritual bankruptcy. A dramatic scene and the use of a colloquial expression account for the success of the verbal irony of "¿Y qué?" There is a contrast, which may possibly be considered a dramatic conflict, between Pablo, lethargic, smoking his cigarettes, and Pedro who is active, continually seeking answers to the question, "And now what?" (PC 272). In the final line Pedro's "So what?" (PC 272) ironically suggests the resolution of the scene. The colloquialism, accompanied in the reader's mind by its characteristic intonation and gestures, at once suggests the underlying meaning. Pedro is no longer earnestly seeking answers but has now discovered, as Pablo knew from the start, that action is of no value. Man's fleeting existence on earth is of no significance, he has no control.

In "Fatiga" (Fatigue), the ironic clash between apparent levity and a message of tragic proportions jolts the reader into intense empathy with the poet's state of despair. Understatement is used in the poem when the poet is told, as if being scolded, to mind his manners: "Sé digno. No te quejes" ("Be dignified. Don't complain," PC 262). In reality, what is at stake is not trifling social convention but the essential significance of life, as the poet tries to escape spiritual death through writing. Finally, pretending to make a promise to be good, he says, "Mas, palabra, algún día me callaré del todo" ("But, take my word, someday you won't hear a peep out of me," PC 263). The poet is again jokingly understating something enormously more important, his inevitable death. These comic twists to the poet's suffering heighten the reader's awareness of his predicament. Here the predominant theme of cosmic irony is death, not tedium. Death to modern man can be considered the supreme source of cosmic irony, for why is man born if he must die and cease to exist? Death devoid of sacred meaning is nothingness and nonbeing. In "Fatiga" there is a double play of cosmic irony; not only must the poet inevitably cease to exist when he dies, but the haunting presence of death in life annuls his possibility of living happily. He trys to escape through money, love, and drinking but concludes: "Y aún me siento cansado. / Quiero decir: me siento. / Y quiero no sentirme, quedarme indiferente" ("And still I feel tired. I mean to say I feel. And I don't want to feel anything, just remain indifferent," PC 263).

Alternation between statements and verbal irony which contradicts what was previously said, enables Celaya to express the intensity of his intuition in the brief poem which follows:

A todo tren
Tiene una querida y un bonito auto blanco.
(A fuerza de ir de prisa

puede figurarse que está enamorado.)
Dentro suyo se escucha
un run-run de dinamo.
¡Mil millones de ceros y mil arcos voltaicos!

Full Speed Ahead

He has a lover and a pretty white car. (By speeding along he can imagine
himself in love.) Inside of him the rrr-rrr of a dynamo is heard. One
thousand million zeros and one thousand voltaic arcs! (PC 275)

From a distant, objective perspective man is pathetically empty,
and the notion of love is just another false pretense in an effort to
escape insignificance. This cosmic irony must be detected by the
reader if he is to experience the despair the poet is attempting to
communicate. Two uses of verbal irony signal an underlying meaning. The comic brightness of the scene, the man, his beloved, and
his pretty white car, fade rapidly upon the realization that the poet
is really expressing the black nothingness of our lives.

A revolt against God is not a frequent theme of cosmic irony in
Celaya's poetry, but does appear occasionally as in "No hay duda de
que tengo un temperamento religioso" (There Is No Doubt That I
Have A Religious Temperament, PC 300). The poet's desperation
leads him to mock the idea of the existence of a supreme being.
Through the use of painful verbal irony the myth of God is deflated
" 'Señor' no tiene nombre, / es un simple pretexto / para alargar dos
puntos de admiración vacía" (" 'Lord' has no name, / it is a simple
pretext / to separate two empty exclamation points"). This ironic
definition of God is especially effective in jarring our emotions because it follows what appeared to be two sincere, traditional invoca-
tions: "Señor, ya no resisto / ¡Señor! me siento roto" ("Lord, I can
endure no longer / Lord, I am broken!"). The desperation of these
lines is strengthened by the ironic definition of God, because it
means that man no longer even has God, his last resort. This poem
reflects the influence of both Miguel de Unamuno and Antonio
Machado in the direct, desperate manner in which it expresses a
loss of faith and anger in the face of God's total silence.

The synthesis of cosmic irony with irony of manner is used effectively, especially in the second section of Los poemas de Juan de
Leceta, "Tranquilamente hablando." In "Cuéntame cómo vives
(cómo vas muriendo)" (Tell Me How You Live [How You Are

Dying]), there is a glaring incongruity between the theme of death and nonbeing, viewed from the perspective of cosmic irony, and the conversational manner of the speaker. Celaya deliberately manipulates the speaker giving him an air of tranquillity and quiet sincerity. Colloquial expressions, "cuéntame," "dime," "ven a mí" ("tell me all about it," "tell me," "come here") and phrases of reassurance, "Yo, también los padezco," "las mías son peores," ("I also suffer from them," "mine are worse"), contribute to the tranquil mood. The use of first person *(yo)* and second person singular *(tú)* verb forms are also important in the establishment of a conversational tone. In the last two stanzas the irony of manner becomes apparent as the speaker's casual calmness is seen to be in frightful discord with what is being discussed:

> Cuéntame cómo mueres.
> Nada tuyo es secreto:
> la náusea del vacío (o el placer, es lo mismo);
> la locura imprevista de algún instante vivo;
> la esperanza que ahonda tercamente el vacío.
>
> Cuéntame cómo mueres,
> cómo renuncias—sabio—,
> cómo—frívolo—brillas de puro fugitivo,
> cómo acabas en nada
> y me enseñas, es claro, a quedarme tranquilo.

Tell me about how you die. Nothing of yours is a secret: the nausea of emptiness (or the pleasure, it's all the same); the improvised insanity of some intense moment; the hope which stubbornly penetrates the emptiness. Tell me about how you die, how you renounce—wisely, how—frivolously—you shine extremely briefly, how you end up being nothingness and you'll teach me, it's quite clear, to remain calm. (PC 287)

Irony of manner in "Con las manos en los bolsillos" (With My Hands in My Pockets) creates a speaker who has some surprising similarities with the type described by David Worcester as the modern descendant of the good-natured, normal, innocent hero of French and English eighteenth-century satires: "They are gray, subdued observers in a world of startling events and startling people. Mild and passive, they are carried along by life's current—sucked into whirlpools, dizzied in rapids, dropped in back waters. Things happen to them; in so unequal a contest what is the use of making an effort? Through their wondering eyes we have a kaleido-scopic vision of a violent, chaotic, and purposeless civilization."[17] In Celaya's poem, the chaos of civilization, "mientras suenan en torno / bocinas distendidas, periódicos idiotas, / voces que rebotan, agrias, en lo hueco" ("while all around swelling horns, stupid newspapers and bitter voices rebounding in the void, ring out," PC 288), reflects the purposelessness of mankind's entire existence. Through irony of manner, Celaya creates a perspective typical of cosmic irony, and the sad conclusion that all human action is futile becomes apparent. The speaker appears to be a calm person, standing with his hands in his pockets, expressing himself in a matter-of-fact way, as is estab-lished through such simple verbal descriptions of his actions as "Vengo y voy, vuelvo y callo" ("I come and go. I return and keep quiet," PC 288). The speaker's low-keyed pose of resignation and indifference clashes with the underlying feeling of intense anguish.

"Fin de semana en el campo" (A Week-end in the Country) is a good example of the combination of cosmic irony and irony of events. A detached, cosmic perspective allows the poet to discover the irony of the human condition. In a world of beauty and tranquil-lity, man alone is the ugly blotch with his repugnant ego to satisfy. Irony of events is used to convey this intuition. Although the poem's speaker says "yo soy un error" ("I am an error," PC 293), there is no verbal irony in his statement. The incongruity is derived from the events themselves, the fact that man's nature is so contrary to the world around him. When the reader senses the contradiction he feels the frustration and despair of man's predicament of being hopelessly trapped in a world where he does not belong.

Entreacto offers one of the best examples of Celaya's use of irony of manner alone. The poet assumes a deliberately lighthearted, clownlike pose (present to some degree in all of the poems). Irony of manner, resulting from the incongruity of the poet's comic manner and the painful emotions being expressed, gives unity to the book. José Hierro has described this characteristic of *Entreacto:* "Perhaps it could be defined as a grotesque formulation of transcendental problems. In this book of Gabriel Celaya there is something clownlike, in its sentimental version, offering the audience a show of diverse articles taken out of a trunk; by means of humor he tries to conceal the pathetic situation. . . . But all the elements he handles with the ability of a juggler are not the least bit funny: they belong to the most profound aspects of life."[18]

In order to enhance his lighthearted pose, the poet includes aspects of different spectacles, especially the circus and the movies. In part VI, "Cine retrospectivo" (Retrospective Movies) for example, the recollections of old movie characters—Judex, Tom Mix, and Charlie Chaplin—conceal emotions of defeat and lost illusions beneath a mood of laughter. The title of part I, "Saltos mortales" (Summersaults) suggests the acrobatic feats of a circus performance. The first poem of this section calls to mind a circus barker, and the fourth, "Acróbatas" (Acrobats) communicates the frightening presence of death hidden in the lights and glamour of a circus act. The title of the book itself is ironic, suggesting a few minutes of relaxation, not painful commentary on human existence.

The feelings expressed in *Entreacto* are only occasionally within the boundaries of the extreme perspective of cosmic irony. In other poems Celaya attempts to communicate a state of melancholic recollection, as in "El niño que ya no soy" (The Child I No Longer Am), and of sadness at the thought of passing time and approaching death, as in "Melancolía de atardecer" (Melancholy at Dusk). The emotions are felt by the poet while deeply involved in living, not from a distant perspective which reveals the absurdity of man's existence.

IV *System Breakage*

Celaya's concept of poetry and his intuitions are constantly evolving; yet he never completely rejects the techniques of a previous period but reshapes them to serve his changing ideas. This is clearly seen in his use of system breakage. Introduced in the first period, it continues to be a successful means of expression in *Los poemas de Juan de Leceta*. "La soledad" (Solitude), in which the break is introduced in the last item of the series, provides us with a good example:

> Cantad, cantad paisajes,
> cantad a Dios, al hombre,
> cantad el mar, la infancia, vuestra amada, los héroes;
> cantad las mil bonitas mentiras de colores.

Sing, sing about the countryside, sing of God, of mankind, sing of the sea, infancy, your loved one, the heroes; sing about the thousands of beautiful, colorful lies. (PC 260)

The positive connotations of the list are not totally negated with the word *mentiras* ("lies") which breaks the system, introducing an object far from praiseworthy. Yet the break is sufficient to contaminate the admirable qualities of the previous objects with a feeling of falseness and worthlessness. The total effect of the stanza is a sense of longing to sing of once-revered ideas combined with disillusionment that such ideals no longer exist.

In another variation, the word which introduces the series and the first member are from the same system, with the following members breaking the established pattern. "Todas las mañanas, cuando leo el periódico" (Every Morning When I Read the Newspaper) relies on several types of system breakage for its effect. The one we are interested in here occurs in the third stanza:

> Levantan sus banderas, sus sonrisas, sus dientes,
> sus tanques, su avaricia, sus cálculos, sus vientres
> y una belleza ofrece su sexo a la violencia.
> Lo veo. No lo creo.

They raise up their flags, their smiles, their teeth, their tanks, their miserliness, their calculations, their stomachs; and a beauty offers her sex to violence. I see it but I don't believe it. (PC 289)

The poet expresses his rejection of the false ideals which capture man's imagination, together with feelings of disgust and dismay. The raising of flags suggests the noble sentiment of patriotism but the feeling changes when the system is broken with the raising of a smile, teeth, and a stomach, adding a progressively more repugnant connotation. The violence suggested by tanks also contributes to the negative evaluation of patriotism, as do greed and calculations.

During the second period Celaya successfully introduces some new types of system breakage, for example, breakage of systems of social convention. All societies have certain generally accepted modes of behavior, and to behave in other ways can be considered a break in the system of behavioral norms. Social conventions are an overt, easily identifiable type of behavior, and a reflection of a deviation from the norm can be used by the poet to achieve an effective means of expression. This type of breakage, introduced in the second period, is especially appropriate for conveying the intensity or uniqueness of a particular emotion or state of consciousness. The following lines from *Las cosas como son* illustrate the forceful reaction which this device can achieve:

> Y al quedarme solo, sólo con su cuerpo
> le tiro del pelo, le muerdo los dedos,
> le soplo en la cara
> le digo: te quiero.

And upon remaining alone, alone with his corpse, I pull his hair, I bite his fingers, I blow in his face, and I say to him: I love you. (PC 324)

The unconventional reaction of tugging at his friend's dead body instead of mourning him with tears or in silence serves to express the intense desperation of the poet in the face of death.

Breakage of established linguistic patterns is another technique introduced during the second period. In the Spanish language, as in others, many commonly used utterances come to function as systems. To change part of the utterance means breaking the system, resulting in important poetic effects. Celaya first uses this type of system breakage during the second period. Sometimes changing the pattern of a common utterance helps the poet to express the complexity of his emotional state, as in the following lines of "Saludo, quitándome algo más que el sombrero" (I Greet People Taking Off Something More Than My Hat) from *Entreacto* (1957):

> Amigo, ¡buenos días,
> buenas tardes, buenas noches,
> buenas melancolías!

My friend, good day, good afternoon, good evening, good gloominess. (PC 542)

The broken linguistic system retains some of the pleasantness and normalcy suggested by the established one which appears first. The poet succeeds in communicating a unique type of sadness, painful, yet not so painful. The selection of this particular linguistic pattern for the expression of these complex feelings is intimately related to the intuition of the poem. Despair in face of life's absurdity becomes more bearable to the poet because it is not he alone who must confront it, but his friends and all men as well. The use of daily greetings exchanged among friends and acquaintances suggests the importance of human solidarity in lessening the painful sadness of absurdity.

V *Visionary Metaphorical Techniques*

Celaya does not abandon visionary metaphorical techniques but they are no longer the sole or primary device as in the first period. Visionary metaphors (comparing something from the realm of reality with something from the realm of fantasy) continue to be used to express both emotions of joy and despair. For example, in *Los poemas de Juan de Leceta*, a visionary metaphor successfully expresses an almost overwhelming, breathtaking sense of joy, the joy of just being alive: "y a veces, en lo alto, mis pulmones despliegan / como flor asombrosa la hermosura del aire" ("sometimes, high up, my lungs unfold the beauty of air like an astonishing flower," PC 290). The following example from *Las cartas boca arriba* illustrates how this *A como* ("like") *B* structure also serves to convey negative, painful emotions: "y me tiendes tu mano floja, rara, asustada / como un triste estropajo de esclavo milenario" ("and you stretch out to me your limp, strange, frightened hand like the sad dishcloth of a thousand-year-old slave," PC 376). Use of discordant sensory perception, a dishcloth capable of feeling sadness, makes *B* a rationally impossible statement. Resignation and humiliation are the emotions evoked by *B*. This metaphor helps the poet to express the complex feelings he experiences when he shakes the worker's weak, timid hand.

Celaya's technical repertoire during the second period also contains visions. For example, in one section of "A Jesús Olasagasti" *(Las cartas boca arriba)*, the poet attempts to convey the spirit of good humor and delightful wit which his friend possesses. After mentioning his devilish jokes, Celaya continues with a line which may seem strangely irrelevant as well as fantastic: "En tus burlas he visto la rúbrica del diablo / y en la luna, brincando, dos caballitos locos" ("In your jokes I have seen the sign of the devil and in the moon two little crazy horses bucking," PC 361). The second verse is a vision, made up of an element actually not part of Jesús' joyful spirit, but capable of expressing the emotion which characterized it.

An innovation in Celaya's use of visions is to string a number of them together in a series, with the effect that each one communicates more precisely the poet's feelings. The author expects that their total effect will express his emotion to the reader. A series of three visions in "Se trata de algo positivo" (Regarding Something Positive) in *Los poemas de Juan de Leceta* expresses a strange sense of beautiful pleasure which the poet has discovered hidden in his subconscious:

> Pero es igual, deliro: rosa giratoria
> que abres dentro mío un espacio absoluto,
> noche con cabezas
> de cristal reluciente,
> velocidades puras del iris y del coro.
> (Solamente—¡qué pena!—estoy un poco loco.)

But it is all the same, I am delirious: spinning rose which opens inside me an absolute space, night with shining crystal heads, pure velocities of rainbow and gold. (Only—what a shame!—I'm a little crazy.) (PC 291)

During the years 1945–1954 Celaya's poetry follows a trajectory between two extremes: from the agony of overwhelming existential anguish to the heights of love and brotherhood. Irony stands out as the most effective technique of the second period. It is supported by innovative use of techniques initiated in the first period: system breakage, visionary metaphors, and visions. *Los poemas de Juan de Leceta* is the most noteworthy book, combining these stylistic devices with a new directness and forcefulness achieved through the use of everyday language and a conversational tone. As the second period closes, Celaya's new concept of poetry as the collective voice of the masses gains in importance, to be followed by a period of complete endorsement of social poetry.

CHAPTER 4

Social Poetry: The Third Period, (1954–1962)

A S the third period opens, Celaya begins to express his faith in the brotherhood of mankind and joyfully senses a new purpose in life. Originally, as expressed in *Paz y concierto* (Peace and Concert), the desire to sing of and to the collective masses is a solution for very deep personal feelings of despair. Paul Ilie in his analysis of Spanish poetry of protest since the Generation of 1936 arrives at a similar conclusion regarding poets' motives for writing. Social poetry really serves no practical purpose, but rather is the result of the authors' attempts to deal with a self which has only fleeting significance. Ilie concludes: "What is left then, is the personal motive, a kind of reassuring of oneself. Social consciousness is the best comforter of a troubled superego."[1] This may have been the unconscious origin of Celaya's social poetry, but there are times during the third period when a genuine concern for improving the conditions of mankind motivates his writing.

During the third period Celaya is concerned with "public" poetry, not with the exploration of the intimate mysteries of life. The themes can be divided into two types: (1) feelings of brotherhood with all men and the expression of their collective anguish and hopes, and (2) poetry of social injustice. Because of love for the poor masses, Celaya becomes more concerned with moving his readers to action against class inequalities. He perceives reality in simplified terms of black and white, and occasionally his poetry during this period is prosaic, a repetition of clichés. Pure aestheticism is rejected as a luxury no longer tolerable in a world teeming with urgent injustices. At the height of his faith in this attitude he declares: "Poetry is not an end onto itself. Poetry is an instrument for us, to transform the world."[2] This belief is exemplified in the poem "La

66

poesía es una arma cargada de futuro" (Poetry Is a Weapon Loaded With Future) in *Cantos íberos* (Iberian Songs).

In the most successful poems of the period, Celaya avoids the danger of sentimental rhetoric and the affected redundance of the social message. A sense of deep human concern for social problems is successfully communicated. The far-reaching and almost absolute power of many of the social and political institutions of our times have made them part of the emotional intimacy of many sensitive poets. The American poet Archibald MacLeish, whose similarities with Celaya have been pointed out by Max Aub and J. M. Navarro,[3] emphasizes the collapse of the barriers between private and public poetry.[4] María Zambrano, referring to the poetry of the exiled writer Arturo Serrano-Plaja, also points to a fusion of intimate emotional states and social concerns.[5]

I *Thematic and Emotional Content*

Twelve books of poetry were written during the third period, half of which could appropriately be called social poetry. In the first and perhaps best of these, *Cantos íberos* (written in 1954), the poet's alliance with the poor masses is associated with the theme of Spain. For Celaya, Spain is in essence the collectivity of the common people, an intuition expressed in "La arcilla que palpo y beso" (The Clay I Feel and Kiss), and "España en pie" (Spain Standing Up). In another poem, "Todos a una" (All for One), the poet urges the people to take part, to be active and construct a future worthy of their goodness. The poet's previous anguish has disappeared; he sings with joy and enthusiasm of his solidarity with the stouthearted common people, reflected in "Hablando en castellano" (Speaking in Spanish) and in "Sancho Panza."

The solidarity and hard work of the humble classes also provide hope for the future in *Las Resistencias del diamante* (The Resistance of a Diamond, 1957), *Vías de agua* (Water Channels, 1960) and *Espisodios nacionales* (National Episodes, 1962). All are long dramatic poems whose settings or events are connected with the Spanish Civil War. In *Resistencias* the story consists of an attempt by four supporters of the Republican side to escape safely by boat to France. Their ally, Mariari, entertains three local civil guards in a bar, enabling her comrades to reach the boat. The four heroes represent the common people but are also marked by individual differences:

Mendía, afraid, hungry, unwilling to die; Arín, always joking; Yarza, tranquil, taking life as it comes; and Vidaur, troubled by the mysteries of life. With the group finally united, weaknesses are overcome and collectively they form a resistance as durable as the facets of a diamond, attacking life with affirmative action.

There is a fundamental disharmony in the social structure reflected in *Vías de agua:* power and money versus the exploited workers. A double obstacle impedes change: the desire of the powerful rich to continue to profit through exploitation, and the passivity of the masses. The death of a student reformer acts as a catalyst for change. The masses, represented in the poem by the *Chapista* ("Metal Worker"), *Jornalero* ("Day Laborer") and the *Contable* ("Bookkeeper"), now understand the difference between good and evil and the possibility of fighting to regain human dignity is suggested. The artistic value of the work is uneven, and at times a redundancy of the message weakens the emotional content.

In *Episodios nacionales,* various scenes from the Civil War are compounded to create a sense of horror and pain. The episodes are of special interest because of their autobiographical nature. Alternating with the war scenes are thoughts about their significance. Suddenly, after the feelings of loneliness, horror and grief reach a climax, a new hope for ending the exploitation of the masses is presented. The abrupt transition weakens the unity of the work and its effectiveness.

II   *"Public" Versus "Private" Poetry*

Cantata en Aleixandre (Cantata in Aleixandre 1959) and *El derecho y el revés* (The Right Side and the Wrong Side, 1964, written in 1962) mark the beginning of a decline in the dominance of social poetry. The social myth struggles against despair and a desire to return to the irrational beginnings of life. *Cantata en Aleixandre* is an interesting experiment in which Celaya combines verses of Vicente Aleixandre with his own to create an original poem. Two forces are at odds: the temptation to explore the mysteries and absurdities of life, and the will to struggle for a better lot for all mankind. Both Aleixandre and Celaya face this dilemma with respect to the nature of their poetry: "In Aleixandre's work there is a basic contradiction, or dialectic, resolved through poetry. Precisely for that reason I believe that what I should write about him is not an essay but a dramatic poem, voicing through different characters (or choruses) the indestructible forces which struggle within him."⁶

The poem is divided into three voices: *Las Madres Primeras* ("The Primitive Mothers"), *Los Otros* ("The Others") and *El Poeta* ("The Poet"). The Mothers embody the irrational, primary forces of life, The Others a positivist, responsible force dedicated to working systematically toward a better future for all.⁷ The third voice, The Poet, finally liberates himself from the realm of the Mothers and embraces The Others' hope of a new community of mankind, singing as one of them and on their behalf.

The theme of *El derecho y el revés* is similar to that of *Cantata en Aleixandre*. The conflicting forces in this poem are represented by the *Ingeniero* ("Engineer"), who works to construct a world which meets man's immediate needs and the *Mono* ("Monkey") who embodies the anguish of modern man's predicament. The latter idly contemplates life, often surrendering himself to immersion in physical pleasures or falling into despair. These two conflicting attitudes exist as a duality in all men and are associated with the mythical figures Prometheus and Epimetheus. The Engineer resists the call of the realm of passion, chaos, and mystery (represented by the feminine figure Ezbá) and successfully awakens the *Zomorros* ("primitive, humble masses") to the need to actively solve the immediate problems of their material existence. The Monkey is not convinced and remains in his world of nihilism.

The content of this long poem is clearly more complex than that of such works as *Vías de agua* and *Episodios nacionales* in which stereotypes of social injustice are presented. *El derecho y el revés* vividly suggests not only the need to improve the conditions of the masses but also the presence of a contradiction in man's nature. The desire for a more meaningful form of life requiring will and action (Engineer) is threatened by a strong tendency to retreat into a state of contemplative inertia or animallike existence. The contradiction is unresolved at the close of the work, for the Monkey is unable to dedicate his talents to the collective cause.

El derecho y el revés is the last book of the third period, the last resounding affirmation in Celaya's poetry of the need to unite and work against social injustice. In *Itinerario poético* (Poetic Itinerary, 1975) the poet explains that *El derecho y el revés* is a key work in his production, representing a painful process of disengagement from Marxist poetry.⁸ Various explanations can be given for the disappearance of the theme of social injustice. First, certain theoretical weaknesses begin to undermine its position. Celaya comes to realize that uniting the common people through poetry is not possible, because their limited cultural access means they will not hear the poetry, or if they do, will not understand it. In the 1960 prologue of *Poesía urgente* (Urgent Poetry), Celaya voices his awareness of this problem: "Access to the masses, without which our poetry was nothing, unless Byzantine, could not be achieved through a literary revolution."[9] Again in 1963, in an interview with Ramón de Garcíasol, he admits this theoretical shortcoming. When asked what poetry can do for the people, Celaya answers: "Directly and at this time, I think, very little."[10]

By 1962, Celaya confesses that it is not possible for him to write only about the problems of the poor. In a letter written to Pablo Vives, Celaya recognizes the complexity of his inner being, the impossibility of escaping ideas and feelings that total dedication to social reform would imply: " 'Like almost all the Spanish writers today,' he writes to me, 'I am a product of the bourgeoisie, and its influence is not easy to erase, in spite of all the efforts made. Frequently, I myself am surprised at the necessity which I experience to write about certain themes or in a style of which I disapprove, without being able to resist the temptation."[11] By the end of the period, Celaya had realized that the theme of social injustice had fallen into clichés—the rich industrialist, and the starving worker. The use of everyday language, which continually moved farther away from poetic diction in order that it might be understood by the masses, was nearing extremes. Finally in 1965, Celaya openly admits his rejection of the theme: "This 'social poetry' thing has tired me a bit. It seems to me a little worn-out."[12]

III New Variations of the Brotherhood Theme: Basque Regionalism

The theme of brotherhood did not disappear with that of social injustice. Toward the end of the third period, Celaya enunciated new variations of the brotherhood theme, of further importance during the fourth period. His most important experiment is *Rapsodia éuskara* (Basque Rhapsody, 1960), very similar to *Baladas y decires vascos* (Basque Ballads and Proverbs, 1965), published early in the fourth period. Because of their likeness, these two books will be considered here together. Guillermo Díaz-Plaja characterizes the content of Celaya's Basque poetry as a profession of faith in the collective soul of the Basque country, which begins as countryside but ultimately includes the behavior of the people.[13] Faith in the collective heritage and living spirit of the Basques fills Celaya with joy, just as faith in social change had healed his existential anguish.

Celaya's characterization of Basque behavior tries to capture its emotional context and motivation, with the result being a portrayal of the spiritual makeup of the people. They are shown as industrious, hardworking, serious, and filled with willpower and drive. These traits form the emotional backdrop for the turn-of-the-century success story, "Crónica de un contratista" (Chronicle of a Contractor), for the contemporary intellectual group, "Los Caballeritos de Azkoitia," and for the traditional games, "Canto a los Juegos Vascos" (Ode to the Basque Games).[14] In *Rapsodia éuskara* from which these poems come, and especially in *Baladas y decires vascos*, Celaya emphasizes the spiritual heritage of the Basque culture over the milleniums, often portraying a magical, mysterious spirit of the countryside as in "Bosques del norte" (Northern Forests) and "Shirimiri" (Misty Rain), which ends with the line: "En mi país todo es magia" ("In my country, everything is magic," PC 1083). In both "La casa de Ursúa" (The House of Ursúa) and "Juan de Alós," anecdotal poems dealing with love, loss of honor, and death, this same air of mystery predominates.

IV *"Private" Poetry of the Third Period*

The third period unquestionably contains Celaya's most strident expression of social poetry, yet even during these years, honesty in examining his own state of consciousness leads him to write poetry of a very personal nature, almost in direct conflict with the forceful extrapoetic pronouncement in defense of social poetry.[15] Love, joy, passion, anguish, or doubt are reflected in Celaya's poems even though unrelated to the cause of social justice. José Hierro recognized as early as 1957 that Celaya, in spite of his statements, was too honest to limit himself to "public poetry" if it did not emanate from his intimate feelings.[16]

Among those books of the third period in which Celaya expresses very private emotions are two inspired by his love for Amparo. Amazement, vitality, and joy are an integral part of the feelings of love expressed in *De claro en claro* (Brightness from Beginning to End, 1956) and *Para vosotros dos* (For the Two of You, 1959). At least momentarily, Celaya finds tender refuge from the arduous task of social change. In *Se parece al amor* (It Resembles Love), from the second period, Celaya lost himself in a world of eroticism, but in these two books love not only brings light and splendor to eroticism but to everyday life as well, which becomes a joyous miracle. With respect to the essential conflict of Celaya's poetry, *De claro en claro*, represents the joyful side: happiness, what life ought to be and can be, a present moment lived to the fullest without the anguish of death.

In "Momentos felices" (Happy Moments) the theme of love and that of the here and now, already expressed in the first period, are united. The five senses become of utmost importance because through them one can experience the extraordinary potential of each moment. The sense of taste is conveyed as the poet's loved one prepares a plate with ham, anchovies, olives, and cheese and brings out two bottles of white wine. The sense of hearing is emphasized in the strophe describing the pleasure of going home at day's end and, in a dimly lighted room, listening to the music of Khachaturian, Mozart, or Vivaldi. Feeling soft breezes, smelling honeysuckle, or looking at girls with sleeveless dresses in the spring delight the other senses.

Para vosotros dos is very similar in tone and themes. Some critics have interpreted the poet's union with his beloved as symbolic of the brotherhood of all mankind.[17] But Celaya makes no real attempt to suggest this interpretation. What he does clearly express in this book is the astonishing capacity of love to transform his life into one of joy. Daily problems, such as not enough money to make ends meet, expressed in "Queremos llorar a solas" (We Want to Cry Alone), and possible depressions, "El viento quiere llevarme" (The Wind Wants to Carry Me Away), disappear and life is faced with a smile, "Mi alegría refleja tu belleza" (My Joy Reflects Your Beauty). Celaya also shares the pleasures of physical union, "Para vosotros dos" (For the Two of You).

El corazón en su sitio (The Heart in its Place, written 1956–1957) and *Motores económicos* (Economic Forces, written 1954–1960), also fall outside the mainstream of social poetry. They contain a type of epistolary poem found in the second period in *Las cartas boca arriba* (Showing One's Cards). The trajectory of this type of poem extends into the fourth period including the section "Algo de lo que debo" (Part of What I Owe) of *Lo que faltaba* (Missing Words, 1967) and four poems of *Versos de otoño* (Autumnal Verses, 1963). The similarity of these poems is confirmed by the second edition of *Las cartas boca arriba* (1975) which includes selections from all the books containing epistolary poetry.

In the early epistolary poems, Celaya attempts to convince his friends not to despair but to become aware of the bright side of life. In later epistolary poetry, especially *El corazón en su sitio*, the poet is less enthusiastic, and a melancholy tone predominates. Now it is not a question of capturing joy, but of prodding his friends and thus himself just to endure life, as is explained in the first poem, which has the same title as the book, The Heart in its Place. Outside exists a beautiful, happy world, but inside the poet's heart is the anguish of nothingness after death.

An examination of the content of *La buena vida* (The Good Life, 1961) will complete our thematic discussion. This long dramatic poem exploring the essence of human existence borders on the philosophical, and once again amid the cries of social justice, Celaya pauses to reexamine the ultimate significance of life.[18] Lázaro, the protagonist in *La buena vida*, returns from death to proclaim the path to human fulfillment: accept death as a natural part of life, live in the present moment, and reject longing for possible immortality. One should be tranquilly content with reality as it is and not hunger for the impossible (PC 801). This message triumphs over the traditional Christian belief that freedom from anxiety is our reward after death, paid for by suffering in this life. The tone is one of joy, perhaps more perfect and intense here than in any other of Celaya's poems.

As Celaya's intuitions for *La buena vida* crystallized, opposing forces became apparent; the characters embody conflicting attitudes about how to deal with the human predicament.[19] The Doctor clings to a belief in some form of human transcendence and sacred values, thus evading a confrontation with death. Marta evades death by losing herself in daily routines; her actions become so automatic that she no longer needs to think or feel. Marta avoids the anguish of death but pays the high price of being spiritually dead in this life. Lázaro unquestioningly accepts death, believing only in the realities of the present. This acceptance brings peace of mind and the capacity to live each moment with maximum intensity.

It should be added that *La buena vida*, like *El derecho y el revés*, is open to more than one level of interpretation, and there are those critics who find social implications in the work.[20] Lázaro is interpreted as the symbolic representation of the masses, who undergo an arousal of consciousness, realizing that their condition will improve only when they make demands for immediate improvements and no longer resign themselves to suffering because of hope of a life in the hereafter.

V *Stylistic Techniques*

The use of dramatic resources, especially dramatic structure and characterization, is the outstanding stylistic feature of the third period. We will include examples from the two long poems of the second period, *Las cosas como son* (Things as They Are) and *Lo demás es silencio* (The Rest is Silence), which initiate Celaya's use of this form, as well as from the long dramatic poems of the third period.[21] *De claro en claro*, *Para vosotros dos*, and *Rapsodia éuskara* provide examples of immediacy of action, another important dramatic technique. Excepting the increased use and variation of dramatic resources, there are few significant stylistic innovations. Contrast becomes of greater importance, including some new uses found in relation to dramatic structure. System breakage and repetition continue to be used frequently, but irony, very effective during the second period, is not present, and visionary metaphors are scarce, usually appearing only in the long dramatic works as part of the characterization of those not concerned with the masses.

Conflict is a fundamental component of drama. Man seeks harmony in the cosmos, and when this harmony is disrupted by conflict, a vigorous emotional reaction begins, becoming more intense until harmony is reestablished. Conflict as the essential component of drama was first emphasized by Gustav Freytag, and then by Ferdinand Brunetière, whose law has become accepted, though some exceptions have been pointed out.[22] Brunetière did not suddenly discover a previously unnoticed characteristic of drama but combined both Aristotle's idea of struggle in tragedy and Hegel's doctrine of "tragic conflict," going beyond them to include all forms of drama. Brander Mathews summarizes Bruntière's theory in this way: "He subordinates the idea of struggle to the idea of volition. And in so doing he broadened the doctrine to include not tragedy only but all the manifold forms of drama."[23] The essential characteristic of drama, then, is the portrayal of the will of a man striving toward a goal, which comes into conflict with contrary forces whatever they may be—fate, other men, social structures, or even inner forces within one person, conflicting ambitions, or interests.

The conflict must be carefully ordered because the primary emotional effect of drama depends on the rising intensity of the emotion stemming from it. The emotional content should be maintained or augmented until the moment of climax, which marks the beginning of the restoration of harmony and the release of emotional tension. Aristotle's beginning, middle, and end are the three basic parts of plot (the ordering and emphasis necessary to achieve the desired emotional response): (1) The presentation of the protagonist's goal and the obstacle which will cause the dramatic conflict. (2) The action, how the opposition and the protagonist's meeting cause the latter to shift and alter his plans, though all his actions must remain logically connected to his original purpose. (3) The resolution of the conflict, making clear whether or not the protagonist reached his goal. Dramatic emotion results from the author's arrangement of events in a closely knit causal system; a chain of events loosely connected would not have the same effect. The author must have a clear purpose in mind from the start, so that emphasis occurs precisely where necessary to prepare the audience for the emotional content he hopes to communicate when the climax and resolutions are reached. Clarity of the protagonist's goal, together with complications, minor crises and climaxes, pointers, and plants, all function to create suspense, or the forward movement necessary to increase the emotional tension in the audience.

Cantata en Aleixandre exemplifies Celaya's use of dramatic structure in the long poems. The basic divisions of beginning, middle, and end can be recognized and contribute to the poem's unity, continually directing the reader's attention to the protagonist's goal. This carefully arranged sequence also maintains the reader's emotional involvement and makes him more receptive to the final solution. The approximate structural divisions are as follows: The beginning (PC 715–22) reveals the protagonist's goal, "Prometiéndoos a todos un mundo iluminado en cuanto yo me despierte" ("Promising all of you an enlightened world as soon as I awaken," PC 719), and the two obstacles, the strong attraction of the irrational world of man's elementary beginnings and rejection by The Others. This early and clear establishment of the conflict is essential to the poem's unity. The middle (PC 722–50) encompasses two units of action. The Poet's liberation from The Mothers and his confrontation with The Others each form one unit, and an escape into the memories of paradise forms the other. The Poet and The Others reminisce together thereby weakening the conflict between them. The middle ends with the climax in which The Others state The Poet's newfound hope: perfect instances of light which will be experienced by living collectively, for and in others (PC 750). The resolution (PC 750–56) elaborates this new form of awareness and hope. The poem ends with the protagonist's death. Having given himself totally to his mission, he dies upon its completion.

In his long poems, Celaya frequently strengthens the unity of basic dramatic structure by using certain techniques. Transition, or the change from one scene, mood, or topic to another, can contribute greatly to the unity of a work. In *Lo demás es silencio*, for example, the Chorus' song, "Corazón, corazón" (Heart, heart, PC 433), is an effective transition between the protagonist's attempt to be the voice of the people and his return to a primitive, chaotic world. The song is a satirical answer to the protagonist's plea for help. It offers some relief after the tense emotional crisis which precedes and makes the protagonist's following change in mood acceptable. In *Cantata en Aleixandre* the speech of The Mothers (PC 736–37) serves as transition between the section dealing with the poet's dual conflict and the paradise section. The Mothers also prepare for the reappearance of The Others, mentioning them and summarizing their attitude toward the protagonist just before they speak (PC 729).

A specific type of transition called preparation or introduction of characters, which generally refers to the first appearance of a character, is also found in the long poems. In *Lo demás es silencio*, Celaya handles the introduction of the Messenger skillfully, avoiding too sudden an appearance and at the same time creating suspense. The first indication that a new character is about to appear is a call from the distance to the Chorus, "Camaradas" ("Comrades"). This call goes unacknowledged as the Protagonist continues his speech. The second call is briefly acknowledged by the Chorus, "¿Quién nos llama?" ("Who is calling us?" PC 452). After the third call, the Chorus becomes attentive to the arrival of this unknown person, and in their speculation about the Messenger some of his spiritual traits are revealed. By the time the Messenger appears, the reader is filled with suspense, wondering if his expectations about the new character will be confirmed.

Lo demás es silencio offers examples of two other important techniques. Forward movement of the poem is enhanced by the occasional use of pointers, something that urges the reader to look forward to what might happen. A good example is found in the beginning section. The protagonist's hope for a world "que pueda llamar mío" ("that I might be able to call my own," PC 415) points toward the Promethean world the Messenger says can be built through unified effort. Plants—some event, object, or dialogue in a drama whose significance is not immediately apparent, but becomes evident as the drama progresses—strengthen the unity. Marian Gallaway points out how this is accomplished: "The audience tends to look backward toward the plant from the latter scene in which its use becomes apparent."[24] After the Messenger has proclaimed his good news, the significance of the Chorus' statement about him just before he entered becomes apparent. Referring to the sound of his approaching footsteps the Chorus had said that they established intelligent borders around chaos (PC 453).

VI *Suspense*

Another component of dramatic structure important in Celaya's long poems is suspense. Suspense is closely related to the general arrangement of materials, and also depends on the other structural techniques. Suspense may vary in kind and intensity according to whether it is found in the beginning, middle, or end, and it contributes to the poem's forward movement. Celaya's most effective use of suspense is found in *La buena vida*. From the beginning to the climax, a chain of pointers creates suspense with regard to the character of Lázaro. Suspense is normally built in relation to the characters in a play. It is a highly effective technique for heightening the reader's emotional response because its effect is not momentary, as is that of surprise (generally related to situation rather than character), but can be sustained from beginning to end.[25] The chain of pointers continually makes the reader wonder: Has Lázaro revealed the whole truth about the nature of death? Suspense is created by the protagonist's inability to remember his past life or his experience of death. Each time this vagueness of recollection repeats itself the reader becomes more anxious to know just what Lázaro really thinks. Suspense is further intensified through the Doctor and Marta's suspicions that Lázaro is hiding part of what he has learned, and they persist in questioning him (PC 785, 796, 798).

Suspense arises out of the reader's uncertainty about Lázaro's experience. It is not just intellectual curiosity, for the significance of the protagonist's experience also affects the reader emotionally. There is a complex interplay of hope, for joy in this life and for some form of afterlife as well, and fear of nothingness after death and of spiritual death in this life. Here the suspense is sustained by the reader's desire to ascertain that what he guesses Lázaro's message to be is really true. A proclamation in favor of accepting death and living happily seems to be the message, but until the climax there is some uncertainty.

Celaya creates another unit of suspense which keeps the reader emotionally involved during the resolution of the conflict. The reader is more at a loss here to know how the Doctor and Marta will finally react than he was at guessing Lázaro's message. Marta and the Doctor continually raise objections to the idea of living only in the here and now: eternal life can be achieved through suffering (PC 807); what Lázaro proclaims leads to a sinful life (PC 808); happiness only lasts for a fleeting moment (PC 810). Will they accept Lázaro's answers to all of these objections? Just six stanzas from the end the Doctor accepts the message. Because of the prior suspense, Celaya has succeeded in involving the reader emotionally and he rejoices with the Doctor's decision.

Another device, complication, consists of "cross currents of action which alter the course of action of the protagonist,"[26] and it can also create suspense. Marta's efforts to have Lázaro return to the normal routine of everyday living, so he can forget his strange, unorthodox message, is a complication which creates suspense. Not only does it keep Lázaro from getting on with the business of clearly defining his message, but there is also the remote possibility that he will follow Marta s advice. Lázaro rejects all of Marta's pleas and a crisis occurs when he lashes out verbally against her. Emotional tension is high and the reader is uncertain how she will react: "Y haces como que existes, mecánica, en la nada. / Vives como dormida. Duermes como viviendo. / Tú, activa, eres la muerte" ("And you pretend you exist, mechanically, in the realm of nothingness. You live as if you were

asleep. You sleep as if you were living. You, so active, are death,"
PC 790).

VII   *Characterization in the Long Poems*

An important part of the effectiveness of dramatic structure in
communicating the affective elements of the poet's intuitions is
characterization. The fundamental conflict of a drama is portrayed
by a protagonist's seeking of a goal. The protagonist is an indispensable part of successful dramatic structure, attracting and sustaining
the audience's emotional involvement in the events which serve as a
focus for the work. Marian Gallaway points out three ways in which
a protagonist can be made to carry out his role in the dramatic
structure.[27] First, he must be characterized as credible; second,
attractive in some way; third, volitional and dynamic.

In *Las cosas como son* Celaya has taken advantage of all three in
his characterization of the protagonist. He is believable because of
the creation of a realistic scene. We can picture him in very concrete
circumstances, standing before the dead body of his friend Pablo.
The protagonist is attractive because he possesses the admirable
qualities of sincerity and honesty, conveyed through the use of
rhetorical questions and naive, innocent statements placed in par-
entheses, for example "(¡Comprenden qué raro me parece eso!)"
("[Please understand how strange that seems to me]," PC 324) and
"al pensar en Dios (¡no puedo evitarlo!)" ("upon thinking about God
[I can't avoid it!]," PC 325). Repetition of certain phrases, "Crean,
soy buen chico" ("Believe me, I'm a nice guy"), also serves to make
the protagonist attractive. By making the goal extremely desirable
and by emphasizing how deeply the protagonist suffers from his
need to achieve it, he is made to appear volitional and dynamic.
Until the goal of spiritual peace and joy is reached, he suffers anguish and is alone and lost in the face of death.

The characterization of the protagonist of *El derecho y el revés*
also contains the three components, but they are achieved in a
slightly different manner. The Engineer is credible because he is
consistent in the way he interacts with other characters and in his
beliefs. That he will think and act in certain ways is already partly
established before the poem begins, because Celaya builds his
character on the framework of the mythological figure, Prometheus.

The Engineer possesses admirable qualities, cleverness and inventiveness, also similar to those of the god Prometheus, and, like an epic hero of the poor masses, he struggles to "emancipate man from servitude," thereby achieving a higher form of existence.[28] The dynamic will of the protagonist is established as soon as he makes his first appearance. His entrance is not prepared for but comes suddenly and without warning, indicative of the forcefulness of his character. The abundance of short exclamations, "¡Corbardes!" ("Cowards!"), "¡Desgraciados!" ("Good-for-nothings!"), "¡Hijos míos!" ("My children!") and imperatives, "Ocupad" ("Occupy"), "Golpead" ("Strike"), "Dad" ("Hit") in the first speech likewise emphasizes his strength and aggressiveness.

Secondary characters also contribute significantly to the structure and emotional effect of the works. For example, the Chorus of *Lo demás es silencio* aids in the exposition, getting the protagonist to state his goal and to discover the obstacle of the pull toward the Terrible Mothers. The Chorus also causes a complication: the protagonist's attempt to find meaning by expressing the chorus' problems. In addition, this collective, secondary character serves as an important link between the conflicting views presented. The Chorus' suffering expressed in the first half of the poem is clearly related to the Messenger's solution of brotherhood and the Promethean creed. Lastly, the Chorus serves to emphasize the Protagonist's position through contrast. Its rapid acceptance of the new myth and quick action, beginning almost immediately to pound the hammer, contrasts with the protagonist's reluctance and half-hearted acceptance of the new message.

In *La buena vida*, Marta is important to the structure of the poem because she embodies the obstacle which temporarily impedes Lázaro from achieving his goal. María is also important as a secondary character for she complements Lázaro's position by being a living example of his good news. The contrast between María and Marta helps to emphasize the traits of each and is especially vivid in their reaction to the just resurrected Lázaro. María is jubilant, reminding him of their past joys and anticipating future ones. She has absolutely no interest in what Lázaro has learned on his trip to the world of the dead, for there is too much living to be done. Marta, on the other hand, is extremely upset by Lázaro's new way of looking at life and is anxious to know what he has discovered.

Celaya uses several techniques to help establish both general and individual traits of the characters. One of these is the selection of names which themselves indicate something about the nature of the character. In *El derecho y el revés*, the connotations of *El Ingeniero* ("Engineer") and *El Mono* ("Monkey") provide an accurate indication of the nature of these two characters. The Engineer wants to build and control the concrete world around him and he esteems the value of work, which beginning with small tasks can become a grandiose accomplishment. The Monkey, on the other hand, rejects rationality, is capricious, and enjoys the physical pleasures of life. *Los Zomorros* refers to some grotesque animal masks used during Basque carnivals. The name helps communicate the animallike, and at times irrational, behavior of this collective character.

Ezbá, the feminine character of the poem, is present in a vague, distant, yet pervasive way through the sound of her voice. Her name is also an important means of suggesting her most common attributes. In the preliminary note, Celaya explains its meaning: "Ezbá to Ez-bay . . . is a Basque name which literally translated means 'yes-no' " (PC 911). *Ezbá*'s promise of beauty and pleasure can be deceiving and lead instead to suffering. She offers soothing sensual pleasures, the unconsciousness and security of the womb, but like a fleeting ghost, she cannot be captured and only impedes man's striving toward a better life (PC 955–56).

Another technique of characterization is the use of different meters for characters according to the type which best expresses their traits. In *El derecho y el revés*, for example: "*El Mono* speaks in short broken verse; *Ezbá* in brief *canciones* ("songs"); *Los Zomorros* in *alejandrinos* ("Alexandrines"), and *El Ingeniero* in eleven-syllable verses."[29] In *Lo demás es silencio* the protagonist's speeches are in long lines (fourteen syllables), which implies a certain gravity. The shorter line of the Chorus' speeches is in accordance with its less philosophical, more practical view of life's problems.

The style of speech of the characters can also serve to reveal what they are like. In *El derecho y el revés*, the lyrical tone of The Monkey's speeches, including many vivid images, "Melancolía, / dorado otoño, / azúcar negro . . ." ("Melancholy, golden autumn, black sugar . . . ," PC 926), "El mundo es el cadáver / de un dios que debió suicidarse / y ahora hierve, descompuesto" ("The world is the corpse of a god who must have committed suicide and now boils, decomposed," PC 930), contribute to the reader's correct perception of his personality. In the same work the animallike qualities of *Los Zomorros*, suggested by their name, are elaborated by Celaya in their speech, sprinkled with meaningless sounds similar to the noises made by animals, for example, "Huy," "A-i," and "juruyu." Celaya also uses this technique in *Vías de agua*. The Day Laborer's outstanding traits are innocence and naiveté. His speech, filled with many colloquialisms such as "llenazo" ("brimfull"), "ni caso" ("not a chance"), and "monsergas" ("silly business"), contributes to the expression of his humble, rural upbringing.

VIII   *Other Observations on the Dramatic Poems*

All of Celaya's long dramatic poems portray the conflict despair–joy. Since conflict is the essence of drama the poet finds adaptations of this form the best means of communicating these particular intuitions. It is also important to note that feelings of joy consistently triumph. This suggests that the poet finds dramatic structure especially suited to express the intuition that the force of joy is so great that it can struggle to victory over despair. The tone of hope reveals the poet's underlying optimism. Man can strive to reshape his attitudes and beliefs *(La buena vida)*, or start by altering his physical environment *(El derecho y el revés)*. Most significant is Celaya's faith that man through will and effort can change his life to achieve a more meaningful existence. Drama is the form which traditionally is based on an underlying belief in free will. Brunetière's theory of conflict as central in drama presupposes a hero exerting his will against obstacles to achieve a specific goal. This leads him to conclude that drama will flourish in epochs when belief in the power of the will is high.[30] Alan Reynolds Thompson also emphasizes that free will is necessary for the dramatic effect. He goes on to explain what he believes to be modern man's reasons for believing in free will, reasons probably very similar to those of Celaya, whose capacity for despair is as great as his capacity for hope: "The traditional view that men are free and morally responsible is not only something we *want* to believe, but something we *must* believe, if we are to find any significance or hope in our lives."[31] It can be said, then, that Celaya's choice of dramatic structure to express an underlying faith in free will is another link between form and content.

Celaya's long dramatic poems, although not intended to be drama, share several characteristics with certain types of drama.[32] The similarities between Celaya's poems and Expressionistic plays are quite evident: both deal principally with inner conflicts and both reveal a high degree of detachment, achieved through the use of long, frequently discursive speeches and the lack of realistic settings to create illusion.[33] The struggles and decisions reached are symbolic of those each man must face in his inner consciousness. In *El derecho y el revés*, for example, there is a struggle between the active and contemplative sides of human nature. Rafael Bosch suggests an Expressionistic tone in *La buena vida*, saying the poem is "reminiscent of the spiritual tone and form of the German Expressionistic theater, as well as of its human and social implications."[34]

The high degree of detachment and the seriousness of purpose of the medieval moralities are also characteristic of Celaya's long dramatic poems. Even more similar is the seventeenth-century *auto* ("Miracle Play") of the Spanish tradition, considered itself by some to be a descendant of the medieval plays.[35] The symbolic use of characters, often based on mythological figures, found in Celaya's poems especially remind us of the *autos*. Angel Valbuena Prat, in his study of Calderón de la Barca's *auto*, *El hombre y la culpa*, points out the presence of universal symbolism: human nature has two sides, one enlightened with the will power to carry out high goals, and one inactive, trapped in the nets of pleasure and self-indulgence.[36] The Engineer and The Monkey of Celaya's *El derecho y el revés* symbolize a very similar duality.[37]

During the 1930s in Spain and other European countries there was a revival of a detached, serious drama, largely related to political and social doctrines. The morality plays of the "new religion" sometimes lacked artistic value and often in a propagandistic manner proclaimed the truth of the Marxist doctrine.[38] Rafael Alberti's *El hombre deshabitado* and Miguel Hernández' *Quien te ha visto y quien te ve y sombra de lo que eras* are two important examples, both reminiscent of the Golden Age *auto*.[39] Three of Celaya's long poems, *Las Resistencias del diamante*, *Vías de agua*, and *Episodios nacionales*, have a blatant social message, and it is very possible that the poet was made aware of the literary possibilities of dramatic resources for presenting the theme of social injustice through the works of Alberti, Hernández, and others, including Paul Éluard.

When found in individual poems of a collection, dramatic resources are almost always combined with other devices and are not the principal source of poetic modification as they are in the long poems. The use of dramatic resources in individual poems occurs most often in the second and third periods, and the best examples are from *Los poemas de Juan de Leceta, Las cartas boca arriba* both of the second period, and *Cantos íberos* the initial book of the third period.

Cantos íberos is a key book in Celaya's production and one of his most successful attempts at social poetry. Many traditional poetic devices are absent; yet others, such as dramatic structure, create the poetic effect. "Vivir para ver" (Live to See) is a good example. Celaya considers what it means to be a poet, and his intuitions are presented in terms of conflicting forces. Some poets sing of beauty and others of human suffering and injustice. Strophes 1–3 serve as a beginning and the discord between "private" and "public" poetry is made clear. The middle (4–16) reveals the essence of aesthetic poetry (the obstacle in the dramatic structure), and it becomes apparent that such poetry will give way to the goal of a morally responsible poetry. Admission by the protagonist that he learned much from the aesthetic masters does increase emotional tension; he is portrayed facing an inner conflict because he recognizes the beauty and value of the artistic poetry that must be rejected. Strophes 8 and 9 present a crisis, and the protagonist directly confronts the irresponsible beings who lack compassion for the poor masses. The climax (strophe 17) occurs when the protagonist makes a definitive break with the poets concerned only with aesthetics. In the ending (strophes 18–23) he turns to his anonymous brothers assuring them of his support. The last two lines emphasize the meaning of the entire poem, synthesizing the conflict and its solution. They also contribute to the unity of the poem, appearing in the introduction as well as at the end.

"All narrative forms make of the present something past; all dramatic form makes of the past a present."[40] These lines of Friedrich von Schiller emphasize another important aspect of drama, that of immediacy of action; the events take place in the present. The structure including characterization enables Celaya to communicate his poetic intuition, aiding principally in two ways: (1) progressive development means he can evoke many varied reactions in the reader, thereby expressing the complexity of the affective component of his intuition, and (2) movement toward a climax means special emphasis is placed on the final image, which synthesizes the multiple variations of the intuition. When the poet's attention focuses on the immediacy of action instead of structure, as it does when he creates brief dramatic scenes, a different poetic end is achieved: the intensity rather than the complexity of the emotion is conveyed.[41] August Wilhelm Schlegel explains how this functions in drama. "The dramatic poet, as well as the epic, represents external events, but he represents them as real and present. In common with the lyric poet, he also claims our mental participation but not in the same calm composedness, the feeling of joy and sorrow which the dramatist excites is more immediate and vehement."[42] Celaya uses the effects of immediacy of action most frequently and effectively in individual poems. Among the long poems in which this dramatic resource is found are *La buena vida, Las resistencias del diamante,* and *Episodios nacionales.*

This technique is most often found in *De claro en claro* and *Para vosotros dos.* The predominant emotion in both books is love, a force so strong that despair is displaced by joy and hope. In "Entre tú y yo" (Between You and Me) from *De claro en claro* a series of alternating stanzas, an eleven-syllable sextet with two tercets of predominately seven-syllable lines, forms the equivalent of a dialogue between the poet and Amparo. The love between them reaches the spiritual depths of the poet, transforming his view of life. The short verses are indicative of Amparo's reassuring presence and the simplicity and intensity of her emotions, which contrast with the poet's more complex thoughts and feelings:

> Versos equilibrados en la punta
> más hiriente y más fina de la aguja.
> ¡Oh paz de los minúsculos sistemas!
> ¡Oh claros descubiertos en la selva!
> ¡Oh momentos puntuados que así salvo!
> Se me ríe y, con el agua, canta Amparo:
>> Tanto tren con tus versos
>> tanto tren
>> dime, Gabriel, ¿para qué?
>>> Mira que te estás matando.
>>> Mira que eres solo un niño.
>>> Sí, Gabriel, que me lo sé.

Verses balanced on the sharpest and finest point of a needle. Oh, the peace of minute systems! Oh, open spaces in the jungle. Oh, precise moments which thus I save! And Amparo laughs and she sings with the water: So obsessed with your verses, so obsessed, tell me Gabriel, what for? Look, you're killing yourself. Look, you're only a child. Yes, Gabriel, I know very well. (PC 641)

The illusion of the immediacy and reality of the scene causes an emphatic response in the reader helping him to feel more intensely the emotions expressed.

"Juntos contra todo" (Together Against the World) is another example from *De claro en claro*. The protagonist is the only one who speaks but because he speaks to the woman he loves, addressing her with endearing terms, "amor mío" ("my love"), giving her commands, "despiértame" ("wake me up"), and asking her questions, "¿qué quieres?" ("What do you want?"), the reader envisions a scene of the two lovers together pondering their difficulties. Because of this illusion of having the man and woman before him as if in real life, the reader feels more intensely all that is said.

"Ya te explicaré manana," (I'll Explain It All to You Tomorrow) is a representative example from *Para vosotros dos*. The almost lifelike presence of the two in the living room looking out the window is very vivid, and serves the purpose of conveying the intensity of the sadness which is about to overtake the girl. In a light, humorous vein the poet suggests in "Queremos llorar a solas" (We Want to Cry Alone) that the joy of love is so pervasive that it is even possible to overcome the difficult domestic financial problems of making ends meet. The scene is more complete than others, with both characters speaking, a third person ringing the door bell, and a moment of suspense. The effect is a sense of happiness that together the lovers can "llorar a gusto" ("have a good cry," PC 767).

In *Rapsodia éuskara* and *Baladas y decires vascos* the use of dramatic scenes is related to the folk tradition. Dramatic techniques have long been a recognized component of folk poetry. For example Ramón Menéndez-Pidal has pointed out the mixture of lyricism and drama present in the *romances* ("ballads"), the most important form of folk poetry in Spain.[43] Dramatic techniques are also found in the traditional folk *jarchas*, the earliest known form of lyric poetry in the Iberian Peninsula. Some critics even associate the development of medieval drama with lyric poetry which embodied dramatic techniques, especially the *debates, recuestas, serventesios, pastorelas.* [44]

Celaya's use of dramatic scenes in his two books of Basque folk themes is closely related then to popular lyricism. Descriptions of the people and their emotions become vivid and lifelike when expressed within the framework of dramatic illusion. In "La casa de Alsúa" (Alsúa's House) in *Rapsodia éuskara,* (PC 852), the father's enumeration of his sons begins with pride but ends in sad dismay because they have all failed him. Here progressive development contributes to the emphasis of the father's final emotional state as well as the illusion that he is standing before us in person trying to explain his predicament. In "Noche de Zugarramurdi" (Night of Zugarramurdi, *Rapsodia,* PC 863) use of a dramatic scene helps communicate the mystery, magic, and superstitions which pervade the emotional make-up of these old mountain people. The technique is even more frequent in *Baladas y decires vascos* including some variations of folk poetry, "Aires vascos" (Basque Breezes) numbers 4, 10, and 15, for example. In others, dramatic scenes convey the intensity of the emotions of the simple people, such as the love and honor portrayed in "La paloma de Jaurguiñián" (The Dove of Jaurguiñián).

IX *Contrast*

Contrast, or antithesis, as it is often called, is a traditional poetic device; it was used extensively, for example, by imitators of Petrarch in the Spanish Golden Age and remains an important technique in twentieth-century poetry. Contrast exists when things are opposed to each other in some way. It helps the poet to express himself with more precision and intensity than normal language because the juxtaposition of opposing concepts means that each one becomes a modifier of the other stressing the outstanding opposing characteristics. Contrast plays a role in several techniques already studied. In Celaya's dramatic poems, contrast is used as part of characterization (Marta and María in *La buena vida* and The Monkey and The Engineer in *El derecho el revés*), and contrasting emotions are the basis of irony. At times it is also an important factor in the technique of system breakage. Contrast appears consistently and in various manifestations throughout Celaya's poetry, but during the third period there is a greater variety of contrast, and we will now examine some of its uses.

Symbolic contrast as a stylistic technique is especially important in *Cantata en Aleixandre* and in *El derecho y el revés*. Celaya makes use of sets of contrasting symbols to express some of his fundamental conceptual-affective intuitions, and these sets of symbols reappear from time to time throughout these poems. The significance of each symbol is expressed more effectively because of the opposing symbol which accompanies it. Perhaps the most important symbolic contrast in *Cantata en Aleixandre* and *El derecho y el revés* is that of masculinity and femininity. The vague spiritual realities symbolized by masculinity, usually stated as *hombres* ("men") or *padre* ("father"), and by femininity, *mujer* ("woman") or *madre* ("mother"), are in some ways rationally related to the sex roles of aggressiveness and passivity, but they go beyond these to reflect two opposing ways of life. Masculinity symbolizes a positive faith in man's ability to progress and, through action, to achieve a better life, whereas femininity symbolizes inactivity and pleasant security, with no possibility of rising to the fulfillment of man's uniquely human potentials. In *Cantata en Aleixandre*, The Others describe man as pulled toward chaos because he is the son of his mother, and driven to build with words and bricks because he is the son of his father (PC 731). In *El derecho y el revés*, The Engineer warns against the dangerous attraction of Ezbá, the feminine character of the poem, describing her as an archaic force against which the men must fight in order to work and build (PC 957).

Another symbolic contrast often used by Celaya is expressed with the symbols *noche* ("night") and *día* ("day") in *El derecho y el revés* and with *sombra* ("shadow") and *luz* ("light") in *Cantata en Aleixandre*. Night and shadow symbolize inactivity related to spiritual suffering, anguish, and death. Day and light, like masculinity, symbolize a faith in man's ability to progress and achieve a better life. The conflict found in *El derecho y el revés* is summed up with these contrasting symbols when The Monkey says to The Engineer "Tu reino es el día / y el mío, la noche" ("Your realm is day, and mine, night," PC 936). In *Cantata en Aleixandre* this symbolic contrast summarizes the warnings The Mothers give to The Poet. He must struggle against the shadows and with the light of his intelligence annihilate the monsters of the archaic world (PC 723). The symbolic contrasts masculine-feminine and night-day express intuitions which seem to continually preoccupy the poet over the years because we find them not only in the books mentioned but also in *El principio sin fin* (Beginning Without End, 1949) and *La linterna sorda* (Dark Lantern, 1964), for example, and in the prose works, *Tentativas* (Attempts, 1946) and *Penúltimas tentativas* (Next-to-the-last Attempts, 1960).

Another manifestation of contrast found in the poetry of the third period is structural contrast, consisting of an opposition between one or more parts of a poem; that is to say, the poem's structure or arrangement is based on the contrast of its different parts. Parts contrast with other parts when each expresses opposing thoughts and feelings. Such differences are often accompanied by contrasting techniques, long meter versus short meter, or cultivated vocabulary versus colloquial speech. "Defendamos nuestra vida" (Let's Defend Our Lives) from *Cantos iberos* is an example of effective use of structural contrast. The emotion of compassion for the poor in the second part of the poem is felt so strongly by the reader because it vividly contrasts with the indifferent, aloof, philosophical attitude toward life expressed in the first part. The opposition is made even more vivid by a contrast in meter, predominately *arte mayor* (lines of more than eight syllables) in the first part and *arte menor* (eight or less syllables) in the second part, and by a contrast in the use of system breakage, frequent in the first part and infrequent in the second (PC 629–30).

Another type of contrast used by Celaya during the third period to make his poetic expression more effective is syntactic formulas of contrast. A common formula the poet uses is *No A, ni B, ni C . . . sino D* ("Not *A*, nor *B*, nor *C . . .* but *D*"), where *sino* also appears as *solo* ("only") or not at all. In this way the complexity of *D* can be successfully expressed because the meaning of the contrasting elements of the formula is synthesized with *D*. In the poem, "España extraña " (Spain the Unique) from *Cantos iberos*, this formula of contrast helps Celaya to express the essence of the Spaniards, singularly different from all the races and cultures which form their heritage (PC 600).

In another formula used by Celaya (*No A, No B, sino C*) or its variations (*No A, No B, Pero C*, and *No A, No B, C*) the precision and intensity of expression is the result of one of two things: either *A* and *B* strongly contrast with *C*, or, although *A* and *B* may contrast with *C* on the objective, real level, their emotional connotations are attributed to C. These syntactic formulas are especially frequent in *Cantos íberos*, and another poem from that book "La poesía es un arma cargada de futuro" (Poetry is a Weapon Loaded With Future) provides us with a good example of this second type. This poem is a proclamation in favor of public poetry which can serve to eliminate social injustice. Because of the absence of certain traditional poetic devices the poem might appear "prosaic" to some critics. Yet its emotional impact is not the result of chance but of devices which modify our normal use of the language. System breakage, repetition, and parallelism combine with syntactic contrast to achieve the effect. In the following stanza the contrast between the negative components of the formula (what poetry should not be) and the affirmative component (what poetry should be) enables Celaya to express his intuition forcefully. Poetry should be of and for everyone and concerned first and foremost with expressing the genuine feelings of all; it should not lock itself into exquisite formal structures or intellectual games:

> *No* es una poesía gota a gota pensada.
> *No* es un bello producto. *No* es un fruto perfecto.
> *Es* algo como el aire que todos respiramos
> y es el canto que espacia cuanto dentro llevamos.

It is not poetry thought out drop by drop. It is not a beautiful product. It is not a perfect fruit. It is something like the air which we all breathe and it is the song which makes room for everything we feel inside us. (PC 632)

Juxtaposition of contrasting styles is also found in the poems of the third period. Celaya's desire to write poetry of authenticity and truth leads him to reject formalism whose worth lies in how something is said, not what is said. Celaya's use of a direct style which simply names the truths is especially evident during this period of predominantly social poetry, but it can also be found in nearly all of his works. There is a note of discord when one speaks of direct poetry, for to name things simply as we do in normal language would most likely mean no poetry at all. Celaya, even when endorsing a simple, direct style, realizes that it is inefficient and does not permit him to communicate unique, intense, and complex emotional states. All the techniques we have studied so far are evidence that Celaya modifies normal language in order to express his poetic intuitions. An important stylistic technique has developed from this incongruity between direct naming and the need to express a complex state of consciousness. The technique consists of juxtaposing the direct naming of an object with a poetically modified description of it.[45] The following verse from "Un día entre otros" (One Day Among Others) from *De claro en claro* illustrates this technique:

> Estamos juntos. Somos
> terriblemente dichosos,
> como el cielo siempre azul, como el espanto,
> como la luz que es la luz,
> como el espacio.

We are together. We are tremendously happy, like the sky, always blue, like fright, like light that is light, like space. (PC 670)

The first two lines state in very plain language how marvelously happy the poet is in the presence of his loved one, but this direct, everyday language is not sufficient to communicate the wonder of his love. The direct statement is followed by a series of visionary metaphors which includes system breakage. By comparing his feelings of love to the sky, light, and space he successfully communicates their expansiveness and force. The feelings of fright which appear so unexpectedly in the series express another element of the poet's emotional state, his awe and wonder in the face of his new found joy.

X Conclusions

The years 1954–1962 mark Celaya's fervent support of social poetry. In all his declarations, many collected in *Poesía y Verdad* (Poetry and Truth, 1969), he defends "public" poetry—poetry which eschews artistic refinement in favor of forceful support of the collective voice of mankind and which speaks stridently for the elimination of social injustice; much of the poetry of the period reflects these aims. The "public" poetry of *Cantos íberos* opens the period, and in *Cantata en Aleixandre* and *El derecho y el revés* the masses are called to build a better future together. Social injustice is presented in bold terms in *Vías de agua, Las Resistencias del diamante,* and *Episodios nacionales.* Yet before 1962 Celaya realized that his poetry would not eliminate social injustice; furthermore, in spite of himself, he could not silence other feelings which were an essential part of his being. Thus, even while his social poetry was at its height, he continued to write of other themes, including Basque regionalism, love, existential anguish, and the joy of a timeless present. Finally, poetry aimed at social change was abandoned. If there were moments during these years when, in dedication to the social cause, Celaya's poetry bordered on the prosaic or propagandistic, there were others when he successfully achieved a conceptual-affective poetic expression through the creation of a poem, not as an object of beauty, but as a unique means of communication, modifying normal language principally with dramatic resources. Other important poetic devices of this period include contrast, system breakage, and repetition. Perhaps these years reveal better than others the complexity of the poet. We see his vitality and capacity to change and grow, making it impossible to simply apply the label of "social poet."

CHAPTER 5

Irony of the Absurd:
The Fourth Period, (1962–1977)

CELAYA'S disillusion with social poetry after his outspoken support might have been sufficient to discourage him from further
poetic creation. But Celaya is a poet of great vitality, who reacted
not with silence but with determination to once again explore the
significance of life through poetry. For about six years, 1962–1968,
Celaya searched for new directions for his poetry. He began the
process by reexamining his early poetry: "It seemed to me necessary
to return to my very beginning and to the original and archetypal
images which had been part of my youth."[1] Thus, important themes
and techniques of the first period reappear in the initial trilogy of
the fourth period: *Mazorcas* (Corncobs, 1962), *Versos de otoño* (Autumnal Verses, 1963), and *La linterna sorda* (Dark Lantern, 1964).
As if uncertain what direction to follow next, Celaya wrote two
books reminiscent of the third period: *Baladas y decires vascos*
(Basque Ballads and Proverbs, 1965), and *Lo que faltaba* (Missing
Words, 1967). He also experimented in *Música de baile* (Dance
Music, 1967) with capturing in poetry the effects of music and finally
hit upon what can be considered the characteristic trend of the
fourth period.

Celaya's most recent poetry is best described as poetry of the
absurd. A distant, ironic perspective reveals life's total meaninglessness. In all seven books written since 1968—*Los espejos
transparentes* (Transparent Mirrors, 1968), *Lírica de cámara*
(Chamber Lyrics, 1969), *Operaciones poéticas* (Poetic Operations,
1971), *Campos semánticos* (Semantic Fields, 1971), *Función de
Uno, Equis, Ene* (Function of One, X, N, 1973), *La higa de Arbigorriya* (Arbigorriya's Fig, 1975), and *Buenos días, buenas noches*
(Good Morning, Good Night, 1976)—irony, the most important

technique, is often combined with dramatic resources, system breakage, direct and familiar language, and at times visionary metaphors. The conflict between despair and hope has not ended, but during the fourth period a desperate tone predominates, with only an occasional manifestation of the continuing struggle to grasp hold of the joys of life.

I Search for New Directions

Celaya returns to the concept of poetry as *conocimiento* or a means of exploring the unknown, the mysteries of human existence. The themes of living only in the present moment, of the peace of the real, material world, and of returning to the archaic beginnings of life, predominate in the first period, also reappear.

The intuition that the secrets of life are to be discovered in material objects is expressed in *Mazorcas*. The title (Corncobs) is explained when the poet writes: "degrano las palabras" ("I dekernel words," PC 965), and refers both to the content—the poet's careful, step by step exploration of the material realm—and to form—short verses arranged pictorially, like kernels falling from the cob.[2] To discover the archaic significance of some minute detail of the material world is to enter the glory of understanding the immensity of which we are a part. Objects which might contain life's mysteries are approached in an almost happy fashion. In "Bajo los plátanos" (Under the Plantain-trees), a perfect moment in the present, with shade trees and soft breezes, suggests paradise. Other times, a lonely forest, the night, a diamond, or the sea is the stepping-stone of the search. The perception of the world expressed in *Mazorcas* resembles certain aspects of the poetic thought found in Jorge Guillén's *Cántico:* "The things of this world reveal themselves as objects, dense in their own being, in accord with their definition, true to their essence. . . . Such a view calls for an awareness of the presence, the immediacy of things in space and the present moment in time."[3] Celaya has acknowledged his continuing admiration for the poetry of Guillén, and critics have noted this influence.[4]

As in *Mazorcas*, feelings of both joy and anguish are expressed in *Versos de otoño*. Discord continues to be a fundamental characteristic of Celaya's poetry. For example, "En Las Landas" (In Las Landas), "En barca" (In a Boat), and "El acto" (The Act) all reflect an optimistic attitude. Joy springs from living intensely only in the present moment and from the wondrous beauties and miracles of the material world. In "Octubre" (October) peace emanates from the discovery that one can eliminate anxieties by relinquishing questions about death and living in the here and now. Despair is prevalent in many poems, however, especially in those which follow in the line of *Las cartas boca arriba*, such as "A José Luis Cano." In some poems Celaya's two worlds, the one of death and anguish, the other of happiness in the here and now, coincide. "Buen retiro" (The Good Refuge) is an outstanding example, and the result is, according to Ramón Barce, "a serenely bitter spark."[5]

In *La linterna sorda*, overwhelming anguish leads the poet to undertake a new exploratory journey, and the discoveries are similar to those expressed in the two previous books. One must live now without a past and without a future, existing in a given moment as things and beasts exist. The primordial world, unspoiled by existential longings, is the real and sacred form of existence.

Since the task of the poet, as now perceived by Celaya, is to discover the latent essence of the world around him, he must attempt to see in new ways, turning objects around and viewing them from strange perspectives. This means a return to the use of visionary metaphors and visions. In "Aventura poética" (Poetic Adventure), Celaya explains that he uses surprising visionary metaphorical techniques because they help capture the hidden essence of things.

In *Mazorcas*, the visionary metaphor, "La soledad, / ojo inmenso" ("Solitude, the immense eye," PC 997) allows the poet to express the fright, helplessness, and near horror which accompany the loneliness of his human predicament. "El establo" (The Stable), provides a good example of Celaya's use of visions in these three books. The poet has discovered in the peaceful existence of the cow an answer to man's anxiety; he must exist only in the present moment as does the entire unthinking material, plant, and animal universe. The idea is accompanied by a feeling of awe, wonder, and peace at having found an answer for mankind's suffering. By presenting a fantastic image of a giant, cosmic cow, the poet successfully communicates these emotions.

Celaya continues to use contrast, and it is often important in achieving the poetic effect in the initial trilogy. In "Lo real" (The Real World, *Mazorcas*) the strong sense of anguish felt by the reader at the close of the poem is achieved through structural contrast. The first nine strophes express the explosive joy of savoring each mo-

ment of life, and the last introduces a sudden contrast, the thought
of the suffering which exists in the world. "Azul" (Blue, *La linterna
sorda*) offers an example of the juxtaposition of contrasting styles. A
poetic elaboration of an intuition is followed by its presentation in a
direct statement:

> Estoy sumido en la verde
> proliferación
> tentacular y ciega,
> en ella,
> soy una larva. No soy

I am submerged in a blind, green tentacular formation, and in it I am a
larva. I do not exist. (PC 1063)

To say "I do not exist" is not sufficient to express what living without
any concept of self is like. Juxtaposed to the simple statement is a
poetic vision which attempts to communicate more vividly the precise feeling.

La linterna sorda is especially interesting because of its innovative
dramatic structure. Celaya carefully arranges the individual poem
on a framework of dramatic structure, including a conflict based on a
willful struggle to reach a goal and the ordering of events to create
movement toward a climax. The unity achieved enhances the value
of the book as a whole, in addition to that of each poem. *La linterna
sorda* is the most successful example in all of Celaya's poetry of this
particular use of dramatic structure. The first poem is equivalent to
the beginning of a drama and establishes the protagonist's identity,
the nature of his goal, and the obstacle he must overcome. The
protagonist, speaking in the first person, represents any man who,
confronting the human predicament, feels anguish and despair. His
goal is to discover the significance of his present life through the
exploration of mankind's beginnings. The formidable obstacle
which prevents his achieving a meaningful life is identified as loneliness in the extreme form of alienation.

The middle of the work, "Fisiología astral" (Astral Physiology),
through the climatic poem "El instante en su punto" (The Precise
Moment), shows the protagonist searching desperately. With great
determination, he penetrates the archaic world. In an effort to reach
an understanding of the meaning of human existence, the

protagonist moves from the cosmic "Fisiología astral" to the inorganic "La sal" (Salt) and "El limo" (Slime), looks at possible transformations among the material world, "Ayuntamientos" (Union) and "Ars Magna," then progresses on to plant life, "Gruta marina" (Marine Grotto), and finally to animal life, "Ovejas" (Sheep) and "El establo" (The Stable). From the point of view of dramatic structure, this sequence of nine poems serves to build suspense. As the exploration moves up the evolutionary scale toward man, the reader becomes more anxious to know whether or not the nonfeeling neutral existence of the material world will reveal a means of overcoming the anguish of the human condition. The protagonist has learned to live only in the present moment: "Neither before nor after, now dizzily still, instantaneous, this moment" (PC 1061). The intensity of the joy which accompanies this discovery is successfully communicated, because the revelation comes at the climactic moment of the dramatic structure, when the reader's emotional tension is at its highest point.

"Azul" (Blue) functions as the end within the dramatic structure and clarifies the protagonist's new interpretation of life. This poem offers a vivid example of the freedom and joy which come from existing only in the present moment. The last poem of *La linterna sorda*, "Epílogo" (Epilogue), falls outside of the structure, unless considered an anticlimax, and deals with the polemic between private and public poetry.

The initial trilogy of the fourth period clearly indicates a break with the previously dominant social poetry. But for about three years following this rupture, 1965–1968, Celaya marked time without finding a new direction for his poetry. Some of his work continued his latest form of collective poetry, that inspired by his Basque origins. *Baladas y decires vascos* is very similar to *Rapasodia éuskara*, the latter written toward the end of the third period. Basque themes allowed the poet to continue to communicate his feelings of oneness with other men while avoiding trite expressions of social injustice.

Lo que faltaba is reminiscent of Celaya's earlier social poetry with the themes of inequality and hunger. As an author he is well aware of the possible shortcomings of social poetry, but as a man he still feels a moral obligation toward those who are treated unjustly. One section, "Algo de lo que debo" (Something of What I Owe), contains epistolary poems like those of *Las cartas boca arriba* and *El corazón en su sitio*. "Cantata en Cuba" is another attempt to revive the cry of social injustice. It was written during Celaya's stay on the island in 1967–1968.

During this brief time of uncertainty regarding the nature of his poetry, Celaya also publishes *Música de baile,* in which he attempts to capture the powerful effect of music.[6] More than any other form of music, jazz possesses the listener and liberates him from suffering. After an intensification of pain, a primitive force gradually begins to take hold. Rational thought ceases, and the listener is only conscious of the music. An innovation in the use of visions is the outstanding poetic device of *Música de baile*. An "extended vision" consists of terms from the same field applied in an unreal, impossible way to a number of objects or to the same object in a number of different ways, forming a group which functions as a unit. Words related to housecleaning are woven into this extended vision from "Jazz, No. 8" which describes the emotional effect which jazz singers have on the poet's spirit:

> y sacuden
> la vida por su nada,
> le quitan polvo y paja,
> le raspan sus cascarrias.

And they shake life by its nothingness, and dust it off and brush away the hay, and scrape off the mud spots. (PC 1135)

II *Celaya's Most Recent Poetry*

Los espejos transparentes (Transparent Mirrors) clearly reveals for the first time the salient characteristics of Celaya's most recent poetry. The poet continues the struggle to understand the human condition. The difference with respect to previous works, accentuated in the six books that follow *Los espejos transparentes,* is that unity with the material realm and the joys of the present no longer provide even fleeting moments of spiritual peace.

As in the second period, Celaya finds irony the most effective means of expression. An extreme form of cosmic irony, irony of the absurd, predominates and encompasses both the content—(the anguish of absurdity) and the form (contrast between comic and tragic elements) of this group of books. With a loss of faith in all absolutes, the perception of purposelessness and irrationality comes to dominate man's existençe. The only conclusion he can sustain, that life is absurd, brings despair. But because human existence is senseless, he cannot even take his despair seriously. Absurdity means that man is caught in a tragically comic predicament, and this type of cosmic irony, frequent in the twentieth century, has evolved its own characteristic literary expression. In the following lines Charles Glicksberg points out some of its most important aspects: "If everything in the universe is absurd, then the boundary line between probability and improbability, the fantastic and the factual, truth and imagination, the real and the so-called unreal, breaks down, as it does in the literature of the grotesque. . . . In those moments of insight when everything is seen as illusion and even words seem a meaningless succession of sounds, the writer of the absurd dissolves in laughter at the ridiculousness of his situation."[7]

Viewing life from this perspective of irony of the absurd, Celaya concludes that man, as a unique entity with feelings and thoughts, does not exist. Life is a dead end; there is no hope. With his human sensitivity totally neutralized, the poet moves one step beyond despair into an exact, insane nonhuman realm. Feelings of anguish gradually move underground until in one of Celaya's latest works, *La higa de Arbigorriya* a desperate, grotesque laughter is the only sound heard. In his seven most recent books, Celaya combines irony of the absurd with irony of manner, a matter-of-fact, objective pose which clashes comically with the fantasies expressed, and tragically with the underlying state of despair. Two other important techniques that complement the use of irony are dramatic structure and system breakage, and like irony both have already made a successful debut in Celaya's poetry. The result of this combination is a very forceful poetic expression and some of Celaya's most original books.

The poet is fascinated with the mysteries of human existence and in *Los espejos transparentes* he presents them as strange, unsolvable puzzles. The delicate, pleasant sensations of *Mazorcas* are gone. "Mecanismo de repetición" (Repetition Mechanism) is a good example of how the poet is now playing the game of exploration in cold blood. The section "Complot II" is a group of eccentric, anecdotal poems which suggest the irrationality of human existence. Everything including religion, "La denuncia" (The Accusation), is a farce, and the poet is alone in a world where nothing has meaning.

The section begins with a quotation from Franz Kafka's *The Trial*, and several poems are reminiscent of that work. In the section "Recintos" (Enclosures), Celaya successfully communicates the nausea an individual feels when he finds himself trapped in an endless labyrinth, perhaps of his own making. The poet uses many details to create an authentic mystery, and repetition, suggested by the title of the book (Transparent Mirrors) is also important. Order, precision, exact rational instructions, numbers, and at times, silence, are all part of the ironic, matter-of-fact pose (irony of manner) which the poet assumes when describing the nonsensical projects.

"La sentencia" is a good example of Celaya's use of irony in *Los espejos transparentes*. The reader's response at the end of the poem is almost one of not knowing how to respond. Ambiguous emotions, both comic and tragic. accompany a desperate feeling of frustration. Seeking explanations to the perplexing situations only serves to confirm the absurdity of life. Irony of the absurd is present in its characteristic form of a lack of boundaries between the real and the fantastic. The poem begins with a description of some quite normal events; the narrator is sought out by a group of friends who take him to the beach for some serious purpose. Suddenly, a fantastic monster is introduced into the realistic scene. In addition, indicating the spiraling effects of irony in this poem, the monster has both real and fantastic features.[5] The discovery of the skeletal remains of a very large water creature falls within the events of the real, but that the creature has such characteristics as elevators in its hind legs and a restaurant in its left knee, is inconceivable. Irony of the absurd also manifests itself as a loss of distinction between the rational and irrational. The use of "then" in the last two lines suggests a logical cause-and-effect relationship between the narrator's actions, condemnation, and reduced sentence. On the other hand, the fact that he should be condemned to die just after undergoing intensive care to save himself from a death he had wanted is somewhat illogical.

In *Lírica de cámara* (Chamber Lyrics) all things which exist are systems of thousands and thousands of minute atomic particles—continually shifting neutrons, protons, and electrons—including man who is not unique in any way. The title (Chamber Lyrics) refers to Wilson's chamber, part of the atom-smashing cyclotron. Man as a human being does not and never did exist. In "Fi-5" the nature of this irony of the absurd is made clear, at the same time it is contrasted with a more traditional type of cosmic irony. The poet suggests that the question Is God dead? is not important, as it once was for his grandparents' generation. Rather, now it is a matter of accepting the fact that man has never been born. The total negation of man's uniqueness is sometimes presented with a wry smile, as in "Mu-5," in which the neutrons, protons, and mesons appear animated, resembling cartoon characters. But such a smile only helps to convey the tragic dimensions of man's predicament. Not even the anguish of nonbeing, nor the despair of absurdity are his, because he is simply a mass of atomic particles. This ironic perspective conveys to the reader a state of depression, total hopelessness and defeat.

The emotional effect of *Lírica de cámara* also depends on Celaya's use of irony of manner. A pose of complete objectivity is established. Often the speaker of the poems resembles a scientist describing his data and conclusions as in the following lines from "Fi-5": "Everything is neutral: equality of peace without evolution," and "I exist. It is evident."[9] In "Beta-4" a series of words and phrases— "indifferent," "insensitive," "acquitted from mankind and his feelings"—have a combined effect of suggesting objectivity. This scientific stance is in harmony with the atomic terminology, and together they give unity to the poems.

For the most part the tone of *Lírica de cámara* is so neutral that the deeper emotional connotations are not immediately perceived by the reader. There is a pause, then suddenly an awareness of the tragic proportions of the poet's intuition. The book is not in the end pessimistic, for underneath the atomic particles beats a very human heart. Somehow resisting extinction, man's heart is still capable of love, and he continues to sense the joy of beauty and the happiness of a present moment. This resurgence of human essence is presented through a sketchy dramatic structure which interrelates two contrasting intuitions about the meaning of life. On the one hand, Celaya encounters anguish, disillusionment, and despair; on the other, the glorious joy of living, free from the oppression of time. The first part of the book, "Alfa" through "Nu," forms the beginning of a loose dramatic structure. The conflict is soon made clear: a desire for all that is human clashes with the obstacle of life viewed exclusively as systems of atomic particles. In "Beta-2" Celaya emphasizes the discrepancy between the atomic vision of life and the

traditional humanistic one. The expression of the conflict is enhanced through the use of anaphora and variations of the syntactic
formula, No . . . , *solo* . . . ("No . . . , only . . ."):

> No hablemos como hombres, sólo como elementos,
> quizá micro-sujetos,
> y aun así pasajeras fijaciones de un campo
> de ondulación perpetua.
> No más cordialidad, sinceridad en ascuas,
> no más humanidad supuesta, ni mentiras.

Let's not speak like men, only like elements, perhaps microscopic subjects
and even then, fleeting fixations of a magnetic field in perpetual undulation.
No more cordiality, sincerity up in flames, no more of this so-called humanity, nor of lies. (LC 16).

The initial portion of the middle section strongly suggests that the
obstacle will triumph, affecting all areas of human existence, especially language, one of man's most distinguishing capacities. Language is ultimately no more than arbitrary groups of sounds, reflecting the breakage and regrouping of man's atomic particles:

> ¿Para qué el nombre?
> Si no existe el hombre
> sobran también los pronombres.
> Lo.
> Ele, eme, ene, tú, Don Nadie,
> uno, ese, otro, ene, che,
> en seguida se convierten en *dramatis personae*
> y no hay dramas,
> ni personas que cuenten.

Why the name? If man does not exist, pronouns are unnecessary. It. *L, m,
n*, You, Mr. Nobody, one, that, other *n, ch*, suddenly they convert themselves into *dramatis personae,* and there are no dramas nor persons worth
anything. (LC 65).

The latter portion of the middle section, "Omega" through "Rho,"
intimates that the conflict is not yet over and the protagonist, representing a humanistic view of life, still struggles for survival. Poems
revealing man's capacity for enjoyment of the beauty of his sur-

roundings, for love, for memories of himself, and even for fear and suffering in awe of the universe, are to be found in this section.

Finally, following "Sigma-1," the book ends in a triumph of the protagonist. With stubborn obstinacy he holds on to what is familiar, rejecting the neutral, whirling realm of atomic particles. The world the protagonist has saved may be a false one, but one in which he can live happily, as is vividly expressed in "Tau-1." The conclusion of the drama is enhanced by the symbolic use of "dog," representing the poet's obstinate determination, like that of an old faithful dog, to keep on being human.

Harmonizing with irony and dramatic structure is Celaya's use of system breakage. Although these three are not the only poetic devices in *Lírica de cámara*—we also find repetition and visions—they stand out as the most important. System breakage, described in detail in chapter 2, is based on a rupture of our normal, logical perception of things. Among the several different types of system breakage in this book is a new variation of breakage of logical systems, which consists of the consolidation of the paradox into one hyphenated word. In "Epsilon-7," "tonto-sabio" ("wise fool" or "foolish wiseman") summarizes man's dilemma: whether it is wise to limit oneself to man's clearly defined capabilities, or whether this wisdom is really foolish, denying one the opportunity to transcend his limitations? The paradoxical combination conveys an emotion of uncertainty and longing. Another new variation is breakage of a system of experience. An event which does not fit into the normal system of our experience can be used by the poet to communicate the intensity of his feelings. In "Mu-5," for example, the strangeness of the sequence of the experiences, pressing a doorbell and having the world ring, helps the poet convey the anguish of wandering aimlessly and failing to discover the significance of his fleeting human existence.

A loosely formulated dramatic structure becomes the principal poetic device of Celaya's next book, *Operaciones poéticas* (Poetic Operations). The goal is to live explosively and insanely in the present to such a degree that the obstacle—the horror and anguish of an absurd human existence—becomes insignificant and even laughable. With great volition the protagonist (the poet) progresses boldly toward victory. The first section, "Transformadores" (Transformers), is an introduction in which Celaya expresses the nature of his poetic expression. He wants to shout, not sing. His verses must "squeal" like reality, not lie about beautiful perfections. Celaya further suggests, in the poem "Mi tiempo: perfecto del imperfecto" (My Tense: The Perfect of the Imperfect),[10] that, although his poetic expression is direct and forceful, it is not without devices to transform ordinary language into poetic language.

The protagonist, having set the stage with this description of his poetry, is ready to begin the struggle of a frank confrontation with life. Immediately we find the poet expressing his way of coping with human existence: "When there is no longer hope, the magic of life in the present moment is discovered" (OP 32). "Vivir es una fiesta" (To Live is a Celebration), the title of one of the poems of this section, is indicative of the poet's attitude. To live is to do nothing in particular, listen to Mozart, play chess, or enjoy the small delights of eating and drinking. A complication is soon introduced, the shame and remorse of carefree happiness when there are so many unfortunate people who suffer. This possible obstacle is dismissed with a simple plea for pardon, and the protagonist continues his joyous course. "La verguenza de ser feliz" (The Shame of Being Happy) summarizes this complication and the poet's reaction to it.

In the third section, "Parade," there is a further complication which modifies the protagonist's actions, moving him closer to the complete realization of his goal. The protagonist receives a lesson on how to live totally absorbed in the magic of the immediate present, for before his eyes passes a parade of people who have learned to do just that. They are young people, hippies and flower children, engrossed in each other or in the tiny beauties of nature, oblivious to their future and their past, and capable of gazing into the distance without thinking about anything. In "On the Road," for example, Celaya presents a carefree hitchhiker who does not worry about where he is going or for how long. In another poem, "La buena noticia, según Bruno" (The Good News According to Bruno), the nature of a perfect human relationship is revealed: casual, not profound, and lasting as long as it takes to make love. The protagonist-poet discovers that a state of placid, indifferent contentment can be found in the most commonplace moments of life. Each poem contributes to the understanding of the protagonist's learning process, and thus to the complete communication of the poet's intuition.

The triumph of the protagonist occurs in section IV,

"Máquinaciones verbales" (Verbal Inventions). He succeeds in focusing, with magnified intensity, on the reality of the immediate moment, and it comes alive with fantasy. The poet floats in an irrational realm bombarded by the objects of nature, fascinated, helpless. Closets, lizards, roses, quartz, crickets—all of reality is magic. It is an elemental, primordial world the poet observes, and viewing it, free from every other preoccupation, becomes his being:

> ¿Qué me permite ver lo que antes no veía,
> oír lo que no oía
> volver al paraíso?
> Que he apagado la conciencia y en lo negro
> brilla el sol original,
> la luz loca elemental
> de lo real.

What permits me to see what I did not see before, to hear what I did not hear, to return to paradise? It is that I have snuffed out my consciousness and in the blackness shines the original sun, insane, elemental light of reality. (OP 72).

Operaciones poéticas ends with the section "Epílogo-moraleja" (Epilogue-Moral) consisting of one poem "Revelo" (The Revelation). The dramatic spell of suspension of disbelief is broken, and the poet walks out on stage to make a personal confession outside the framework of the structure. He presents his comments in the form of an anecdote with a moral, which contains the same fusion of the real and the fantastic found in *Los espejos transparentes*. The story is of a man who makes an apparently easy ascent toward heaven after killing the watchman at the first gate, but he ends up taking the dead man's place waiting to be killed by the next person called. The poem can be interpreted as the poet's comment on the content of *Operaciones poéticas*. The seemingly spontaneous, carefree joy of the immediate present is deceiving. The poet's marvelous interpretation of reality is actually a mask to cover the painful tragedy of a meaningless, absurd existence.

"Revelo" confirms that Celaya depends not only on dramatic structure to achieve a poetic effect in *Operaciones poéticas* but equally on irony of the absurd. This perspective means that all the poems of the book, while on the surface exhibiting feelings of joy, contain a residue of tragic despair. Throughout the book, Celaya hints that his obsession with the magic of the present is rooted in desperation, and at one point he confesses, "My defense is laughter and a cynical insanity" (OP 19). The essence of Celaya's poetry, the conflict despair-joy, is still very apparent. System breakage complements the use of irony and dramatic structure, jolting us into perceiving the intensity of the joy of exploding in the immediate present.

Campos semánticos (Semantic Fields) offers another confrontation with the world of the absurd. Celaya experiments with the irrational disintegration of language and with the pictorial arrangement of the text on the page. There is an obvious reminiscence of Dadaist techniques, and the book is dedicated to Tristan Tzara, founder of the movement. On the surface many of the poems appear almost incomprehensible. The poet plays with strange picture puzzles whose irrationality makes the reader smile wryly. Yet the poet's game is really a desperate shout in the midst of the anguish of an absurd existence. "Los signos" (Signs) and "Pizarra nocturna" (Nocturnal Blackboard) are good examples of Celaya's use of irony in this book. *Campos semánticos* is an extreme experiment, and, although the pictorial poems are fascinating puzzles, the disintegration of language is so exaggerated that the poetic impact is weakened.

In *Función de Uno, Equis, Ene, F (1. X. N.)* (Function of One, X, N), the only reality which exists is one of brightness, velocity, perfection, and total indifference, and man must fuse with the mysterious order of a universe he will never comprehend. Beyond fury, sin, happiness, and pain, all one can do is to exist in neutral light and burn out.[11] The distant, ironic perspective is no longer formulated in terms of nuclear physics, as in *Lírica de cámara,* but in computer codes, which explains the formulalike title of the book. "Uno" ("One") is the individual; "Ene" ("N"), the collectivity of men; and "Equis" ("X"), the incomprehensible order or divinity which governs all existence. Why does the poet choose computer language? Exact and impersonal, it creates the perfect pose to speak coldly and objectively about the total lack of meaning of human life. In many poems the irony elicits laughter, with the computer spouting strange sounds such as "juy," "gi," and "yaj." One of the best examples of this use of computer humor is in "Mécanica oral" (Oral Mechanics). Dialogue, or the formulation of the poem in alternating voices with the computer being interrogated, also often intensifies the comic effect.

Función de Uno, Equis, Ene reflects one of Celaya's most acute moments of despair. His pessimism is so great that he prefers to live as a nonthinking, nonfeeling flash rather than as a human individual. In "Estrépito para no oír" (Clamoring in Order Not to Hear), for example, vague memories of human essence (in the form of a friendship) resound like a dying echo, contrasting with the whirling forcefulness of a neutral reality. The last poem, "Dedicatoria final" (A Final Dedication), however, reveals Celaya's ever-present duality. Just like the little dog wagging its tail at the end of *Lírica de cámara* to symbolize the hope of unique human essence, the poet ends *Función* with a note of tenderness. In a poem dedicated to Amparo, he expresses very warmhearted feelings of love and childlike joy.

In *La higa de Arbigorriya* (Arbigorriya's Fig), Celaya no longer suggests total absorbtion in the present moment as in *Operaciones poéticas* or the neutral existence presented in *Lírica de cámara* and *Función de Uno, Equis, Ene*, but rather here steps into a funny, insane world. The poet explodes in "noisy, irrational, grotesque laughter" because nothing makes sense or has meaning.[12] Here the laughter is much more jocose than in previous books. It seems that this louder laughter hides a deeper desperation and emptiness—no causes, no hopes, just absurdity. Celaya has described *La higa de Arbigorriya*, explaining that it is like a "final break with everything, saying, well nothing makes sense, everything is idiotic. I'll just sit back and laugh like a clown."[13] The poet's essential conflict of despair-joy is clearly evident. There are indications throughout the book that the wild happiness of the protagonist Arbigorriya is a means of escape, and by the end the poet says: "Don't you understand by now that this endless laughter covers horrors?"[14]

It is a mature poet who has reached the stage of strident laughter, and he now looks back at the events of his life from an extreme ironic perspective, presenting humorous autobiographical sketches of different phases of his youth. The first section "Vida y milagros de Arbigorriya" (The Life and Miracles of Arbigorriya) opens with several poems of this type including "Nacimiento" (Birth), "Infancia" (Infancy), and "Niñez donostiarra" (Basque Childhood). The last section includes, for example, a poem recalling an uncle, "Ingeniero progresista 1900" (Progressive Engineer 1900), and another, his father, "Arbigorriya recuerda a su padre" (Arbigorriya Remembers His Father). Irony enables the poet to criticize cultural values, such as the "progress" of the nineteenth-century industrialists, and to mock the absurdities of society, including useless wars, as in the following lines from "Niñez donostiarra": "The winds flutter like a frightened angel; after all, two wars are still needed for perfect happiness" (HA 23). Celaya was a small boy during World War I and here, referring laughingly to his childhood days, says that World War II and the Spanish Civil War were needed for perfect bliss. The ironic verses suggest the absurdity of masses of men killing each other.

Irony of manner, in which the poet feigns a nonchalant attitude or a normal situation to hide the painful side of life, is successfully combined with irony of the absurd. A variety of "normal situations" serve as the basis for the ironic effect in these poems, for example, an advertisement in "Aquí del allá" (The Here of the Beyond): "Learn to be stupid in only seven days" (HA 69); or instructions to a child in "Biografía" (Biography): "Don't drink. Don't smoke. Don't cough. Don't breathe" (HA 84); or the routine of a doctor's office as in "El piel-roja examinado" (The Redskin Examined): "Take off your skin. I want to examine you" (HA 81). In still other poems, Celaya makes use of the forms of a telegram, "Arbigorriya habla del amor" (Arbigorriga Talks About Love), and of a recipe, "La lata de vivir" (Canned Living). All of these situations are reminiscent of the irony of manner found in *Los poemas de Juan de Leceta*.

A synthesis of irony and dramatic technique results in an especially successful group of six poems subtitled "Interrogatorio" (Interrogation); "El timbre de alarma" (The Alarm Bell) will serve as an example. The circumstances are apparently real: officials question an individual suspected of political subversion. The use of dialogue here is one element of irony of manner, employed to suggest the routine of police interrogation. Certain phrases used by the interrogator serve the same purpose: "Do you realize that you almost provoked a revolution?" (HA 39); "Tell us your party affiliation" (HA 39); and "Explain yourself more clearly. Act normal if that's possible" (HA 40). The prisoner is Abigorriya, and his absurd statements clash with the apparently real situation, causing laughter. With a straightfaced attitude he says: "¿No podría hablar con Dios? Es mi abogado, ¿comprendes? / Yo quisiera casarme con una bicicleta. / Sólo El sabe la manera de burlar qué lo prohíbe" ("Couldn't I please speak with God? He is my lawyer. Understand? I would like to marry a bicycle. And He is the only one who knows how to get around what prohibits it," HA 40).

The interrogation in this poem becomes increasingly less comprehensible until the climactic moment when "Confusion General S.A." ("General Confusion, Inc.") reigns in the entire city. A structure resembling that of drama gives unity to the poem. The protagonist's goal is to convince the authorities, the obstacle, of the reasonableness of the irrationality of his acts, thereby gaining freedom. In the end, the last three strophes, the absurd world of Arbigorriya triumphs with lunatics and judges killing each other. In the midst of the confusion, Arbigorriya calmly asks the guard for permission to leave to take care of an urgent matter and picking up his hat, walks away "tan-tran-tran tranquilamente como el mismísimo Dios" ("so calm-calm-calmly just like God himself," HA 42). The poem is indeed humorous but the joke is on the reader because he is left to deal with an absurd existence.

In addition to dramatic structure and dialogue, Celaya also uses characterization to create the ironic pose. *La higa de Arbigorriya,* unlike previous works, has one character with certain traits which gradually evolve, and his presence gives unity to the book. The initial poem introduces us to Arbigorriya, and we learn that he is the poet's double. In *Los poemas de Juan de Leceta,* Celaya previously had created a double of this type whom he described or talked with in order to reveal intimate facets of his own being. The technique is amplified here, with the character appearing in almost all of the poems of the book. Arbigorriya is a mischievous clown, symbolized by his name which means "carrot" in Basque. At the same time Arbigorriya displays innocence and naiveté, and is often an unknowing victim of the will of others. In some ways he reminds us of Charlie Chaplin, but he certainly is a little more crazy. The following verses from "Peligro de la inocencia" (The Danger of Innocence) summarize some of Arbigorriya's outstanding personality traits:

> Le detienen. Le multan. Le pegan. Es un santo
> que aún vive sin entender por qué le tratan así.
> Y ante su risa de idiota, yo me siento avergonzado.
> Si él abriera su sombrilla subiría, recto, al cielo
> mirando sin ver, mirando lo que nosotros no vemos,
> entre un suspiro y un ¡oh! millonario de ceros.

He is arrested. He is fined. He is beaten. He is a saint who still does not understand why they treat him that way. And in the face of his idiotic laugh, I feel ashamed. If he were to open his parasol he would go straight up to heaven, looking without seeing, looking at what we do not see, between a sigh and an "oh!," millonaire of zeros. (HA 29).

These qualities endear him to the reader and the poet's desperation is felt with greater intensity precisely because of the attractiveness of the character.

In *Buenos días, buenas noches* (Good Morning, Good Night) the poet is still convinced of the absurdity of the human predicament, but the insane laughter has been silenced and the anguish transformed. That delicate inner balance between joy and despair once again shows signs of shifting to the positive side, for the poet has learned to face the awesome spectacle of existence tranquilly, and even feel uplifted by it. In previous poems, *Lírica de cámera* and *Función de Uno, Equis, Ene*, submersion in an indifferent, nonhuman world was a desperate attempt to combat life's absurdities. Now a sincere, stoic acceptance of his insignificance and unexplainable lot as part of an abysmal universe brings peace to the poet. All human ideals and efforts—humanist, Marxist, or Promethean— accomplish nothing. Man is too unimportant. All one can do is accept the astonishing neutrality of reality: "La locura del mundo que nada sabe del hombre, la indiferencia feliz. / No la justicia. La paz" ("The insanity of the world that knows nothing of man, joyous indifference. Not justice, peace").[15]

The feelings expressed are much closer to resignation than jubilance. The quality of happiness reached is not as exuberant or complete as the joy expressed in books of the first and second periods when the poet still had hope of discovering some meaning in life. But one of the conclusions of those early poems, living only in the present moment, is similar to what Celaya now recommends. Experiencing the trivial everyday things—suggested by the title of the book (Good Morning, Good Night)—without illusions of transcendence is what a peaceful life is all about. The fact that the poet is able to reach this state of tranquillity after the despair of the preceding five books confirms his tremendous and continuing struggle to cling to life's precious joys.

The second part of the book is entitled "Refugios," and the poems are less optimistic, revealing feelings of fear and a need to find a warm, cozy human-sized hiding place from the "sin-fondo" ("abysmal depths"). The poet comments on human behavior. Why all the projects, causes, and dreams if such activities are meaningless? The answer is that men need to find their own personal refuge—tombs, monuments, dreams, empires, books—to survive the awesomeness of reality. The change in the emotional content of *Buenos días, buenas noches*—the poet's resignation to live serenely—is accompanied by a change in technique. Irony is less important, and Celaya relies largely on simple, direct language. He creates a tone of sincerity and conversational intimacy—similar to that found in *Los poemas de Juan de Leceta*—through the use of direct address, rhetorical questions, and exclamations, resulting in a forceful expression.

We also find excellent examples of various types of system breakage—paradox in "Matinal" (Morning), breakage of linguistic patterns in "La vida es ancha" (Life is Wide-open)—a few instances of irrational metaphors and visions—"Lo abierto" (Openness)—and several kinds of contrast—juxtaposition of contrasting styles in "Ante el sin-fondo" (Facing the Abyss), simple contrast in "Dentro y fuera" (Inside and Outside), and fixed patterns of syntactical contrast in "No la justicia, la paz" (Not Justice, Peace). Celaya adds another of his preferred devices to the repertoire, repetition. A greater use of regular meter—fourteen-syllable lines are frequent—and rhyme is perhaps related to the mood of tranquil resignation. Regular meter is more frequent in the first part than in the second, in which feelings of fear reappear. The rhyme, which generally does not follow a totally regular pattern, is assonantal and occurs internally as well as at the end of verses. The repetition of the same rhythms and vowel sounds helps convey the awesome exactness and peace of the nonhuman world.

III   *Conclusions*

During the fourth period, 1962 to the present, Celaya experimented, searching for new directions after the exhaustion of social poetry. His first experiment is the trilogy, *Mazorcas, Versos de otoño,* and *La linterna sorda,* which reveals certain similarities with works of the first period, including the themes of joy in the present moment and union with nature, and the frequent use of visionary metaphorical techniques. After a brief time of indecision and a return to social poetry, Celaya made a second attempt which definitively achieved a new direction for his poetic creation, in many ways reminiscent of the tendencies of the second period.

Irony is the characteristic form of expression. It is similar to that of *Los poemas de Juan de Leceta*, but now more extreme, consistently reflecting the distant perspective of irony of the absurd. The basic intuition is one of despair. Life is meaningless and the only way to survive is to reject human essence and exist neutrally like atoms *(Lírica de cámara)*, flashes of light in the present *(Operaciones poéticas)*, and computer codes *(Función de Uno, Equis, Ene)*, or laugh insanely *(La higa de Arbigorriya)*. Feelings of hope and authentic joy appear to succumb to the poet's resignation; life is absurd. Yet the positive emotions have not disappeared. They flicker from time to time, especially in *Lírica de cámara* and *Operaciones poéticas*, and dominate in the first part of *Buenos días, buenas noches*, demonstrating that Celaya's vital struggle between despair and joy is even present in his mature poetry. Other outstanding stylistic techniques, also originally introduced in the second period, include dramatic structure and system breakage. Direct, everyday language, visions, contrast, and repetition are also present. Celaya continues to be a prolific writer, and the seven books of poetry written since 1969, with their innovative use of irony, and synthesis of techniques successful in earlier poetry, are among his most original.

CHAPTER 6

Prose Works

G ABRIEL Celaya has earned his place in the history of Spanish literature primarily as a poet, and his more than forty books reflect a broad range of tendencies. His creative vitality has moved from Surrealism, to Existentialism, to social poetry, and most recently to irony of the absurd. At times Celaya's enthusiastic search for the form which most precisely communicates his intuitions leads him to experiment with other genres. We have already seen indications of this in the long dramatic poems which combine elements of drama with those of lyric poetry. Celaya has also expressed his creative vitality in prose works, the most important of which are five narratives. Two can best be described as collections of fables, *Tentativas* (Attempts, 1946) and *Penúltimas tentativas* (Next-to-the-last Attempts, 1960). The others are novels, *Lázaro calla* (Lazarus is Silent, 1949), *Lo uno y lo otro* (One and the Other, 1962) and *Los buenos negocios* (Good Business, 1965).

The narratives express Celaya's own personal philosophy of human existence, and his preoccupation with the intellectual content somewhat weakens the aesthetic value. Yet it is precisely this content that makes these works of interest, because the ideas presented are very similar to the themes which consistently reappear in his poetry. The narratives reinforce the thesis that Celaya's works reveal an essential unity above and beyond the variety of their themes and styles. Conflict, the basic element of Celaya's most important poetic techniques and of the content of his poetry, especially in the fluctuation between states of despair and joy, also plays a fundamental role in the philosophy of existence presented in the five narratives.

Celaya has written a drama in prose, *El revelo* (The Revelation, 1963), similar in many respects to the long dramatic poems of the third period. He also has published several long essays. Four of

113

these deal with literary theory and techniques, *El arte como lenguaje* (Art as Language, 1951), *Poesía y verdad* (Poetry and Truth, 1960), *Exploración de la poesía* (Poetic Exploration, 1964), and *Inquisición de la poesía* (Poetic Inquisition, 1972). These essays are of special interest because of their relationship to his poetic expression. Other prose works include a collection of traditional children's rhymes, *La voz de los niños* (The Voice of Children, 1972), which reflects Celaya's interest in folk poetry, and *Bécquer* (1972), a history of the life and works of the Spanish Romantic poet, Gustavo Adolfo Bécquer, which contains many of the same conclusions about Bécquer found in *Exploración de la poesía*. Some one hundred thirty articles which have appeared in newspapers, magazines, journals, and as prologues complete the list of Celaya's prose. These articles deal principally with literature and other art forms and contain little of significance not expressed elsewhere in Celaya's prose.

I *Narratives*

The form of the five narratives varies greatly, from a fablelike presentation including figures from Greek and Christian mythology, to novels with contemporary settings, sometimes very realistic, and even autobiographical. Yet a careful reading reveals a remarkable similarity of themes. Celaya is preoccupied with communicating his intuitions about the meaning of human existence and the path one must follow to reach fulfillment. He is not a disciplined philosopher, and there are areas of his thought which remain imprecise or contradictory. Nonetheless, it is possible to summarize certain central ideas, and it will be helpful to do so before considering the works individually, because each narrative reflects to a greater or lesser degree the poet's essential discoveries about life. The three basic concepts contained in Celaya's intuition are: history, "the other," and optimism of the here and now.

Celaya believes that to live authentically one must become and remain aware that part of his being is already determined by history, by all men that have existed before him. With the technological advancements of the twentieth century, individuals have strayed away from the "primary forces." Modern man fails to recognize that prehistory, timelessness, chaos, and the world of pulsations and sea abysses are part of him. At one time the "primary forces" existed in a paradiselike state with the union of the feminine ("Terrible Mothers") and masculine (archetypal heroes of strength and volition). Since the hero's first exodus from the primary realm, these two forces have remained severed and represent a conflict in man's nature. The "Mothers" embody the emotional, sensory, static unconscious of man's spirit; the hero, his active, rational side. There is a constant dynamics between these opposing forces, and either extreme leads to a false existence, because both are part of man's authentic historical being. If the self *(yo)* of the hero blinds him, the "mothers" become "terrible" and destructive in order to awaken him to his erring ways. If he is weak, the "Mothers" become creative, encouraging his action.

History is part of man's being in still another way. There is a collective unconscious which causes man to relive the experiences of archetypes from all the important periods of history. There are moments in a man's life when spiritually and psychologically he is prehistoric, Greek, medieval, Christian. Celaya compares this spiritual process with that of the development of the fetus which passes through all the stages of the biological evolution of man: cell, reptile, fish, mammal, and finally man.[1] The reliving of archetypes is suggested only in *Tentativas* and *Penúltimas tentativas*.

Celaya believes also that a meaningful life can be achieved only when one comes to the realization that he exists not as a "self," but as part of "The Other," the whole of mankind. Men share a common history, and individual consciousness must die to be replaced by one which acknowledges the interrelatedness of all men. At the same time, in an ongoing process in the present, each individual by his actions is forming the generic man of the future, and therefore his behavior affects all other men as theirs does him. To fulfill the "essential adventure" of creating man of the future, the acceptance of the historical "given" and the interrelationship with others must be reflected in one's actions in the present.

Modern man has lost sight of the essential elements of his being. He is spiritually dead and mechanically complies with daily routines. Many men are aware of this condition because some remnant of the heroic forces leads them to dissatisfaction. Celaya's intuition is optimistic because, beyond the initial awareness that life is absurd, it offers a process of revitalization which can lead to a new and authentic human existence. To overcome despair, the individual must return to the subconscious "primary forces," and by understanding their role and that of "the other," it is possible to reach fulfillment in the here and now. The process can be described as a conflict between the "self" and the authentic essence of man. If "self" is defeated, the goal of a meaningful existence can be achieved.[2]

From the initial pages of the first narrative, *Tentativas*, and especially in the sections "Origin" and "Epodes," it is apparent that Celaya is familiar with the works of Friedrich Nietzsche. The influence of Goethe becomes evident in "Tentativas románticas" of the same work. Celaya still possesses his collection of these authors' works, which he says he read enthusiastically for the first time at age sixteen.[3] In broad terms, Celaya describes them as representing two opposite poles. Although both reveal great vitality, the Spanish poet conceives of Nietzsche as an overflowing of exuberance, "a vital force, a total sundering, the will for power, completely pagan and anti-Christian," and Goethe as limitation, control, and constant, precise activity.[4] These two concepts are reminiscent respectively of the feminine and masculine forces described by Celaya. More specifically, Celaya's embracing of the potential joy of the immediate present is similar to Nietzsche's descriptions of the here and now, and both writers also describe man of the future.[5] From Goethe's *Faust*, Celaya borrows the concept of the "Mothers."

A number of other writers from diverse fields have also played important roles in shaping Celaya's ideas. The writings of the psychologist Carl Jung influenced the poet. When as a young man in his twenties he first began to read Jung, Celaya was greatly impressed with the idea of a collective unconscious. The intuition that man relives the great myths and archetypes of the past is based on his knowledge of Jung.[6] Existentialist thought also was crucial to the formation of Celaya's intuitions. For example, the belief that the "self" cannot reach fulfillment existing alone but only in an interrelationship with "the other," reflects Martin Heidegger's "to be with," and the tedium and despair of the first phase of the renewal process resembles the anguish expressed by Jean-Paul Sartre. The disappearance of "self" as necessary for fulfillment in Celaya's philosophy reflects a familiarity with Eastern religious thought. We have already discussed the importance of this influence in our examination of the themes of the first period.

II Tentativas

During 1936–1946, Celaya spent much time pondering the meaning of his life, and many of his conclusions are found in *Tentativas*

(Attempts, 1946). The intuitions of those ten years of thought serve as the basis for future narratives and poetry. In the prologue of a later anthology, Celaya stressed the importance of *Tentativas* in the evolution of his writings: "Perhaps the reader may not understand why I insist on discussing such a forgotten book as *Tentativas*. But *Tentativas* not only represents a long period of my life—that of my isolation—it also contains a synthesis of all my most fortunate poetry."[7] The work reveals a very careful organization which includes a division into four *tentativas* ("attempts"): "Tragic," "Romantic," "Aesthetic," and "Historic." Each section contains three fables and is introduced and concluded by a brief prose poem.

In "Tentativas históricas" (Historic Attempts"), Celaya describes the heroic action of three mythological figures (Narcissus, Orpheus, Oedipus) who separate themselves from the formless mass of the "primary forces," struggling to reach man's highest potential. These fables reveal the importance of the heroic impulse to begin the renewal process, and at the same time warn of the failure which ensues when the "self" grows out of proportion. A new consciousness of "self" makes it impossible for the heroes to return to the comfort of the "Mothers." Nor do they find fulfillment in their ventures because they have still not learned to recognize the importance of History and "the other." They are isolated and trapped.

The ancient hero disappears from "Tentativas románticas" (Romantic Attempts), and the individual is now portrayed as the anonymous antihero of modern times. In the first part, The City, the lamentable state of man is suggested. He now lives in an urban setting whose center is a gigantic mechanical clock. Man is spiritually dead, and unthinkingly executes his duties with great precision. Anesthetic routines prevent him from fulfilling his essence. The individual or "One," as he is referred to, senses the absurdity of this life and finally, with a vague reminiscence of the heroic spirit, is able to begin searching for a more meaningful existence. The exploration of One's subconscious is portrayed as a trip down a river and through the jungle to the sea. The trip, described in the second part (River) and the last (Sea), emphasizes the need to return to the "primary forces." There is an episode in which drums are heard in the jungle, and One arrives at a village where natives are dancing in the snakelike formation of Yacu-Mama. One desires to join in but does not, saying, "I would divide the serpent. I would not be another link in its body, but rather its head."[8] This statement expresses Celaya's belief that the ancient, irrational side of man's nature must be accepted. One encounters no easy salvation, yet upon returning to the city he sees things very differently, a sign that the renewal process has begun. Though not able to accept the primitive side of his nature, he is at least aware of its existence.

In The Garden and Kaleidoscope of "Tentativas lúdicas," (Aesthetic Attempts), man has moved far away from his origins. With a background of crystal towers, the scene is the palace of Francelisa, who symbolizes beauty and artistic achievements. The characters of "Tentativas lúdicas" no longer carry on the passionate, Romantic struggle to understand life, but like the Modernist and Symbolist writers, limit themselves to the pursuit of absolute beauty and aesthetic perfection. The protagonist of "Lúdicas" is an adolescent readily impressed with what he sees in Francelisa's palace, and anxious to escape the anguish of his search, joins the refined, courtly group. In the last part of this section, The Barbarians, the family history of Kanpotar, the leader of a group of nomads, is described. With heroic volition the tribe attacks Francelisa's abulic palace to awaken the people from their false dreams. This invasion suggests a return to the ancient conflict between the feminine and masculine forces.

In the fourth section "Tentativas históricas" (Historic Attempts), Celaya incorporates Christian mythology into the three fables entitled, Genesis, Incarnation, and Condition. There is continuity of characters from the previous section with Francelisa and Aitzarrak (Kampotar's son) producing a son. Pallido, one of the gentlemen from Francelisa's court, sees in the child hope for the future. Pallido (whose name changes to Ermitaño) carries off the child, Ka. Their adventures in the desert express the conflict in man's nature between the spirit and the flesh. This struggle is not only part of Christian mythology, but is also related to Celaya's intuition of the clash of the masculine and feminine extremes of the "primary forces," the Ermitaño or Hermit representing the purely intellectual side (the rational, masculine hero whose "self" often comes to dominate), and Ka, the unconscious, material, sensory side. Celaya proposes that these two opposing forces must unite in order to give birth to a superior being. In the fable the Hermit dies and Ka, a Christ-like figure embodies both spirit and flesh. Like Christian doctrine, Celaya's personal philosophy of existence contains an element of hope.

In the final part, Condition, Juan, the protagonist, undertakes a trip which symbolizes his search for a meaningful existence. He travels to Europe and with the gradual acquisition of great amounts of knowledge, his "self" grows out of proportion. He becomes linked with the Devil, like Don Juan of José Zorilla's *El Burlador de Sevilla*. In the end the creative forces of the Mothers, now expressed in his love for Inés, and in Christian terms, for the Virgin Mary, intervene and save him from death. The fable makes the lurking presence of spiritual death visible, reminding the reader of the importance of recognizing the "given" that exists outside the "self" both in the present and the past.

At times, *Tentativas* is somewhat cumbersome to read. This is especially true of the last section because the fictional figures represent Christian myths which in turn are used by Celaya to express his own personal philosophy. Another difficulty is created by the gaps and inconsistencies in chronological order. The author's use of continuity of characters and his comments about periods of civilization create a false anticipation in the reader that the fables will follow a logical progression in time. If the work is interpreted as a description of steps toward higher levels of existence, this difficulty diminishes in importance.

In *Lázaro calla* (Lazarus is Silent, 1949) what first calls our attention is the realistic, contemporary setting; but surprisingly, despite the disappearance of the timeless, mythical world of *Tentativas*, Celaya continues to express the same intuitions. He explains that originally the content was conceived of as a fifth section of *Tentativas*: "These 'Tentativas mínimas' ["Minimal Attempts"] became *Lázaro calla*. The fable approach no longer suited me, because precisely what I wanted was to write about something much more realistic. It was the influence of Existentialism."[9] Lázaro, the protagonist, works at the Iribarren paper factory. His life is monotonous and his wife Marta sees that no detail of the daily routine is overlooked. Lázaro is spiritually dead. Functioning like a machine, he methodically complies with the patterns of society. But one day Lázaro sees, as if in a sudden flash of light, the absurdity of all his duties and projects; his total existence is absurd. As do the mythical characters of *Tentativas*, he feels the need to break away from his deadening surroundings and to struggle toward a more meaningful level of existence. He abruptly resigns from his position at the factory. This liberating action allows him to sense the exalting joy of human fulfillment, and he sees the world in a new way: "The simplest things are so marvelous! It seemed to him that he was seeing the world for the first time with virgin eyes. Things as they are, nothing more, but so surprising!"[10]

The first phase of the journey is difficult, for Lázaro is now aware of the anguish and absurdity of life but is still uncertain of what path to follow. The protagonist wanders from the office to his home, and the familiar setting beckons him to escape despair by taking refuge once again in the daily routine. Lázaro longs for Marta to awaken from her stupor and accompany him in the struggle for significance. He cuts the yarn she is knitting, but the "wandering corpse" only reacts by tying a knot and continuing to knit. One of Marta's purposes in the novel is to represent everyday routine, seen clearly in the scene just described. She also portrays the creative side of the Mothers, helping Lázaro to begin his process of renewal. The couple embody the conflict of the masculine and feminine forces in man's nature. Lázaro comes to represent the hero, the intellectual, the "self," like the Hermit of *Tentativas*, and Marta, the unconscious world of flesh and matter. The narrator of the novel describes this difference: "Woman, anonymous, a species, is instinctively the enemy of man, personal and heroic. Womankind is more ancient than man; fabulous, indefinite, primordial. Man, a recent creature, struggles to survive."[11]

Lázaro makes love to Marta and after copulation finds himself completely dominated by her. Gradually he falls into a subconscious state and approaches death. There are no reasonable explanations for man's existence and the narrator asks: "Why did he want to keep on living? What was he still hoping for? The masculine force of creativity which had maintained him whole and unique had volatilized. But he still had his flesh: vague islands of sensitivity; inconsequential cramps; bunches of palpitating cells; formless life which in reality was no longer his life but that of anonymous and blind matter that negates the individualizing effort of man."[12] Marta's dominance of Lázaro and his subsequent death represents Celaya's belief that if modern man is to rediscover a meaningful existence he must return to his origins. Thus Marta's role is creative because she allows Lázaro to begin the process of renewal. Lázaro's death symbolizes the death of the "self."

The action of the novel is minimal, and takes place within the twenty-four hours beginning with Lázaro's resignation in the morning. Interwoven with the slow-moving, realistic events are many discourses by the narrator in first-person plural, referring to "we, mankind," or in third-person singular, referring to the protagonist. These discourses, which resemble the prose of *Tentativas*, afford the author the opportunity to express his personal philosophy directly. Unity is maintained because the discussions always relate to the plot. Yet that perfect balance between form and content necessary for aesthetic success is not achieved. Nor does Celaya accomplish a harmonious blend of the cognitive and affective content; the former heavily outweighs the latter.

Penúltimas tentativas (Next-to-the-last Attempts, 1960) utilizes the point of view of a protagonist who has reached fulfillment. Celaya recapitulates the entire renewal process, emphasizing for the first time the final state of joy in the here and now. Perhaps the greatest achievement of this book is the way in which Celaya has superimposed the existential growth of an individual, the protagonist, with the different stages of development of Mankind. This superimposition is essential to Celaya's intuitions regarding authentic human existence. One must be contemporary, living in the present and simultaneously embody the timeless myths of Man which eternally return.[13] The author succeeds in expressing both an atemporal and historic concept of time.

The book opens with the protagonist's memories of his origins; from the sea he was cast upon the sands. In the core of Man's being there is a link which unites him with the milleniums that passed before he was born as an individual. The sea symbolizes the archaic world of Mankind, at the same time that it suggests the amorphous, material side of the protagonist's being. Abandoned on shore, Man is blindly active, resisting the pain of loneliness and the temptation to return to the primary forces. The "self" grows in its desperation to survive; some unknown heroic force sustains the individual. He works without a purpose but advances, blow by blow, exploring the unknown, soon mastering his domain of "skills." By adolescence, the protagonist has made important discoveries. He recognizes that "the history of each minute, psychological man is the history of Mankind with a capital letter. And this understanding of how History lives in us and how each of us makes History, is then the only adventure that matters to him."[14] He relinquishes his "self" and is now aware that his interrelationship with others brings meaning to life.

In the final section, "The Here and Now," the mature protagonist, a contemporary clearly resembling the author, breaks with the absurdly stupid routine of the factory—like Lázaro in *Lázaro calla*—because he now has another possibility, that of living in the "Eye." The "Eye" allows man to overcome the "dead-end alley" of "self" and teaches the exuberant joy of feeling, seeing, forming the real world of the here and now.[15] It puts the individual on his mark, and the protagonist has now found his mission in life, that of a writer. His rediscovery of the world with the joy and wonder of a child's eyes represents the completion of the process of self-examination. The "Eye" also represents a new stage in the development of Mankind, which according to the author, twentieth-century man is just beginning to experience: "Perhaps man is called upon to become a creature as different from Man today as we are different from the animal we once were in our prehistory. Perhaps the anguish of death is nothing more than a symptom of the maladjustment between the individual and the species or a frustrated rebellious attempt of the 'I' against the 'we.'"[16]

III   *The Remaining Novels*

Lo uno y lo otro (One and the Other, 1962) is perhaps Celaya's most successful narrative because of the unity of form and content. The structure of the novel (like that of a detective story) and the role of each character are essential for the communication of the author's intuitions. The autobiographical narrator-protagonist, Gabriel, is the top executive of a factory in San Sebastián. He is bourgeois and responsibly, if not enthusiastically, fulfills his obligations. As the novel opens, something has interrupted the normal routine. Gabriel and his friend Fernando are carrying out a mysterious undercover mission for some high government officials. Uncomfortable without any explanations, Gabriel reluctantly agrees to associate with a man named Bernabé to see what he can find out. Bernabé, his wife Trinidad, his lover Gloria, and his friends, Dalia, Isaías, Carlos, and Garcián, form a very nonconformist group by Gabriel's standards, who reports the following to the director of covert operations: "All those people do is get drunk and talk about literature. They don't even let me get my work done at the factory."[17] Gradually Gabriel participates more in the group's gatherings and orgies, confessing one night that he too admires Bernabé. Finally he becomes involved to such a degree with the group that he resigns his position with no plans for the future.

Gabriel's feelings are ambivalent. He is attracted to the group but senses a need to separate himself from them. In the end he breaks all ties; as the novel closes, the narrator-protagonist begins a new life as a writer. The detective plot is carefully brought to a close with Gabriel discovering that the group's strange activities are related to helping Laforgue, a political activist called an "ultra," to cross the border. The assistant minister is extremely pleased with the information and tells Gabriel that his mission is completed.

The theme of the novel is the confrontation of One (the rational "self") with "the other," all that exists outside the "self," including mankind's history from its irrational beginnings through the archetypes which have appeared during different stages of civilization. "The other" also comprises the rest of mankind with whom One coexists during his life time. The "self," represented by Gabriel, comes into conflict with the archaic, subconscious realm, portrayed by Bernabé and his friends, with their drinking, dancing, and sex orgies. As Gabriel joins the group he becomes detached from his position at the factory, a symbol of the rational "self." Structurally, the author presents this gradual change by alternating the setting of chapters between the office and Gabriel's meetings with Bernabé. The responsible employee whose alarm sounds at eight o'clock sharp, contrasts with the wild partygoers who idle the time away and ignore obligations. As the immersion of the "self" in the chaotic forces becomes more complete, the office scenes are less frequent, finally disappearing. This contrast of settings also serves to express the conflict between the rational and irrational forces of man's nature.

By the time Gabriel submits his resignation, he has become immersed in the "primary forces," the first step in the renewal process. To achieve a meaningful existence, one must make an affirmative return to an active life. Gabriel's break with the group, who remain in chaos, and his determination to write a novel represent the completion of the process. The detective-story structure makes for entertaining reading, but more important, it is a device which enables Celaya to express the themes of the novel successfully. F. Everette Rosemond has pointed out the intricate relationship between the plot and the theme of self-exploration: "To know one's self is a personal and individual task. For this reason Celaya places Gabriel in the complex network of discovering the secret of the group. Of course, if the group is his subconscious, no one will be able to tell him what his inner secrets are, and for that reason the detective-story plot lends itself perfectly to the search."[18]

There are two separate plots in *Los buenos negocios* (Good Business, 1965), and both reflect important autobiographical events. One traces the historical development of the Iribarren company—resembling the Ramón Múgica firm—over a period of some eighty years. The other, which spans a two-day period, July 26–27, 1951, alternates with the historical chapters and describes the contemporary state of the enterprise and members of the family.

The principal character of the "Crónicas" (Chronicles), José León Iribarren, combines tireless drive with his talent for knowing just which risks will be profitable. From the humble position of a carpenter, he rises to the head of his own large firm. When the founder dies there are two sons, Jesús and León, and a son-in-law, David Muller, to carry on. León is the protagonist of the contemporary setting. Intellectual games, centering on the importance of "self," and enjoying the comforts and status of his economic position form the basis of his existence. Now a man over sixty, he continues to seek sexual pleasure. So great is his obsession that he does nothing to prevent an accident to his wife, believing that her death would allow him to live idyllically with his lover Magdalena. Luisa, León's wife, recovers from her first accident only to become a living example of the spiritual death which invades the Iribarrens' lives, as she mechanically carries out her household duties. She is a constant reminder of the necessity of beginning a thorough process of self-examination.

The contrasting spirits of José León and his son León suggest those of two mythical figures, Prometheus and Epimetheus, already used by Celaya to characterize the differences between Gabriel and Don Valentín in *Lo uno y lo otro* and between The Engineer and The Monkey in *El derecho y el revés*. Like Prometheus, José León has robbed the gods of their fire and wants to build a perfect world. Prometheus, through hard work and suffering, erects order in the chaos. He is saved from the anguish of introspection because his heroic affirmation of life fills the emptiness of whatever doubts might arise. Jesús, David Muller, and his son Jacob Muller follow the Promethean spirit of José León. They continue to dedicate their energy to the family industry. Yet the heroic vitality has diminished and at times it seems that the creative force has degenerated into an automatic compliance with predetermined obligations.

León represents Epimetheus, the tragic counterfigure to his twin Prometheus. Epimetheus admires the works and spirit of his brother and would like to imitate him, but by some trick of fate, the heroic impulse is lacking and all his efforts turn out backward. Celaya's description of Epimetheus also fits León: "Instead of obeying the simple orders of a work done collectively, believing himself better than the others, he thinks and rethinks the absolute importance of his 'self' or sings of infinite suffering. . . . Prometheus the creative titan, willful and positive, becomes Epimetheus, neutral scientist or vague dreamer and introvert, plagued by grotesque transcendentalisms."[19] In addition, just as Epimetheus succumbs to Pandora's evasive sexual attractions, so León is attracted to Magdalena.

These two mythological figures come very close to the masculine and feminine forces found in the other narratives. Prometheus–José León is the heroic, individual, masculine force, freed from the archaic chaos and instinctively and energetically struggling to form a "self." Epimetheus–León is the feminine side—sensual, irrational, static, close to the primary forces, containing both the destructive and creative powers of the Mothers. León's dark, destructive side causes him to do nothing to prevent Luisa's death. Yet this death is also a creative sacrifice which initiates a process of renewal in the Iribarren family. If the "self" dominates (José León), man cannot achieve fulfillment, nor can he if he succumbs to "idleness and nihilism" (León).[20] Both Iribarrens lack the perfect balance to reach toward the highest human potentials. The ending of the novel suggests that there is hope for renewal, and the optimism is conveyed by the decision of David Muller (the great-grandson of José León) to abandon the firm and become a Franciscan monk. The boy has consciously examined his life, reading materials from Saint Thomas Aquinas to Marx, and has discovered his vocation. The humanitarian aspect, rather than the religious, is emphasized, suggesting a new consciousness of "we."

IV *Similarities of Themes of Celaya's Narratives and Poetry*

One of the defects of the narratives—the excess of intellectual speeches by the narrator and other characters—also embodies one of their greatest values, the forcefulness with which Celaya emphasizes his intuitions. Regarding the repetition of certain ideas,

José Domingo suggests a similarity between Celaya and Miguel de Unamuno: "In this respect he reminds us of another illustrious Basque who wrote essays in his novels, undefensible as such, although valued for their ideas and their archetypal characters, symbols more than creatures of flesh and blood; we are referring of course to Don Miguel de Unamuno. Like those of the latter, Celaya's characters repeat his ideas time and time again in a monotonous declamatory style which the author takes care obstinately to hammer out, and the result, which is at times brilliant and efficient with respect to ideology, can flow into falseness and disproportion."[21]

The thematic content, which Celaya so emphatically repeats in the narratives, is closely related to many of the intuitions expressed in his poetry. In the latter there is no elaborate presentation—rather, the poet focuses on some particular aspect of his philosophy, communicating with precision and intensity its emotional as well as its conceptual nature. In several books of the first period—*La música y la sangre, Avenidas,* and *El principio sin fin*—Celaya captures the experience of union with the irrational, erotic, feminine forces. More than feelings of joy, the union provides a refuge from despair; but it also prevents man from reaching his highest potential. This failure resembles the idea in the narratives that immersion in chaos is only the first step in the renewal process. The miraculous joy of *Objetos poéticos* is equivalent to the final state when One has become aware of the "given" of human existence and lives each present moment to its fullest. The belief that joy can only be achieved through annihilation of "self" is also expressed in *Objetos poéticos.* To a large degree then, the essential thematic content of *Tentativas*—except that each individual relives all past ages of mankind—had already been presented in the poems of the first period.

The same year that Celaya published *Lázaro calla* (1949) he also published *Las cosas como son.* The contrasting emotions of anguish and joy expressed in each, respectively, are not as unrelated as might first appear, if we remember that *Lázaro calla* represents the initial stage of the renewal process and *Las cosas como son* the end result. During the second period another aspect of Celaya's intuition, the interrelatedness of all men, receives great emphasis. In *Lo demás es silencio* there is a dramatic struggle between the consciousness of "I" and that of "we," and *Paz y concierto* expresses the joy and fulfillment of the total disappearance of "self" and the birth of a feeling of union with "the other." Again Celaya first expresses his intuitions in poetry; the complete renewal process is not elaborated in the narratives until *Penúltimas tentativas* (1960).

The third period, in which social poetry predominates, coincides with the dates of the narratives which stress the role of "the other" in One's life and in the formation of Mankind. The newly discovered "we" of *Penúltimas tentativas* and *Lo uno y lo otro* is the same "we" of Celaya's poetry which defends the masses and calls for social change. The similarities between the content of the narratives and the social poetry reinforce the idea that Celaya's defense of the downtrodden is not boarding a political bandwagon but a reflection of his personal philosophy, reached after a long process of introspection.

La buena vida has a special relationship to *Lázaro calla* because it was originally conceived of as a prose sequence to the latter. The resurrection of Lázaro in *La buena vida* represents the joyous completion of the renewal process that was begun in *Lázaro calla*. Two other books of the third period, *Cantata en Aleixandre* and *El derecho y el revés*, reflect another aspect of Celaya's philosophy, the struggle between the masculine and feminine forces. The sense of resignation in the face of absurdity, which has come to dominate the last and most important books of poetry of the fourth period, has not been elaborated in narrative form (heretofore reserved by Celaya to express an optimistic interpretation of human existence).

V *Drama, Essays, and Other Prose Works*

Dramatic techniques are an important part of Celaya's poetic repertoire. It is not surprising, therefore, that toward the end of the third period while writing predominantly long dramatic poems, he should try his hand at a play. The result is a brief, one-act work entitled *El revelo* (The Revelation, 1963). The play is mildly satirical, and the humor provided by the everyday problems of the fantastic characters makes it entertaining. At the same time, the work is enlightening, stressing the defects of a conservative, conformist society. Perhaps the greatest danger in such a society is the death of man's spontaneous creativity. The characters are symbolic, including Don Máximo, a talking statue representing the conservative viewpoint; a devilishly playful lost soul who moves on roller skates balancing himself with a red umbrella; a good angel who rides around the park on a bicycle; the park policeman who is ready to suppress any novel behavior, and a young couple in love. In spite of the lack of action, the wittiness of the lines and the fantastic qualities of the characters enable the author to present vividly the essential conflict without becoming rhetorical. Conservative, conformist mentality clashes with an impractical, free-spirited concept of life. The play ends on an optimistic note with conformity loosing ground to man's free spirit, suggested by the young couple who float off the stage as the curtain is lowered.

El revelo has only been produced on two occasions, in 1971 in Santa Cruz de la Zara, province of Toledo, and again in 1973 by the *El Pueblo* theater club of Madrid. The latter production received a very favorable review in the newspaper *ABC:* "The farce came off pleasantly without weak spots. It is one of the most worthwhile works to be presented of those that figure on the already long list of the club *El Pueblo. . . .* It was applauded very enthusiastically by a full house of young students, who formed the vast majority and were, more than a theatergoing group, a group of judges."[22] In his only attempt at playwriting, Celaya has successfully readapted his use of dramatic techniques in poetry to create a brief drama totally appropriate for stage representation.

Celaya has published four works, *El arte como lenguaje* (Art As Language, 1951), *Poesía y verdad* (Poetry and Truth, 1960), *Exploración de la poesía* (Poetic Exploration, 1961) and *Inquisición de la poesía* (Poetic Inquisition, 1972), in which he presents his ideas about the nature of poetry. He insists that poetry is essentially communication. Some types of poetry, especially the purely aesthetic which strives to create absolute beauty, may be limited because the communication function is lost. Regarding form, Celaya stresses that poetic language is different from the everyday use of language because of the element of novelty and surprise. Only by expressing himself in a surprising way will the poet succeed in communicating to the reader or the listener his precise intuition. Celaya also emphasizes in both *Poesía y verdad* and *Inquisición de la poesía* that the established rhythmic and accentual patterns of the common language are as valid a base for forming the musicality of poetry as are the traditionally accepted meters, which for the most part are composites of smaller feet. In our brief examination of Celaya's essays the salient points of his concept of poetry will become apparent.

El arte como lenguaje reveals in its title the fundamental thesis of the essay. Art, referring to literature, music, and painting, is language, or in other words, a form of communication. The artist has something inside of him that he wishes to express. It is an attempt to strike the same emotional chord in another person. Celaya emphasizes the importance of the spectator as well as the author, saying: "Art, in effect, is not enclosed or engaged in works of art. It passes through them like a current. It consists precisely of this flow from one individual to another."[23]

Another point which Celaya makes is that art must respond to two contrary demands, aestheticism ("the pure") and tremendous sensitivity ("the impure"). Perfection of artistic techniques has its limits because of the danger of the poem becoming hermetic. Likewise if a work flows too naturally, spontaneously, and effusively from its emotional source, it will become nothing more than animal sounds. Celaya believes that *both* elements are necessary, and concludes: "The work of art is not a thing; it lives, it represents the drama of the unformulated that we would like to express and which when formulated or captured perfectly becomes incommunicable."[24] To communicate, a work of art must hit upon the exact language which allows these two forces to remain in balance. And that is why Celaya holds that in art, form and content are totally inseparable. If a word of a poem, a touch of the brush of a painting, or the note of a musical composition is changed, the message is changed.

El arte como lenguaje includes sections which describe Celaya's understanding of artistic language. The artist must continually invent his language, in contrast to the common, ordinary language which is given. The artist does not communicate in a habitual, conventional fashion, but by surprise. If the artist could say in everyday language what he wants to express, the work of art would have no purpose for existing. Celaya emphasizes that "artistic language is of value precisely to the degree it is indestructible."[25] It says something unique that cannot be expressed in any other way.

Poesía y verdad consists of some sixteen short essays, nearly all of which had previously been published as prologues, statements in anthologies, or as articles in newspapers and literary journals. The book was published during the height of Celaya's social poetry and can be described as an explanation and justification of his bold, realistic style and a defense of "responsible" poetry. It should be kept in mind that *Poesía y verdad* represents only one stage in Celaya's evolution, and that the statements about poetry are generally more extreme than the poetry itself. In "Respuesta a *El correo literario,*" Celaya says, "Social [poetry] . . . in reality is nothing more than an euphemism to designate that indignation, repulsion, and shame that one experiences faced with the reality in which he lives."[26] The essay "Nadie es nadie" ("Nobody is Anybody") explains the interrelationship of Celaya's sensitivity to unjust social conditions and his existential feelings of unity with others. He is a poet of the here and now, at times embracing reality with joyful affirmation, as is evident in "Digo, dice Juan de Leceta" (I Speak, Juan de Leceta Speaks), the prologue to *Las cosas como son.*

In addition to these statements about the content of the poetry of the third period, the essays also contain a defense of realistic style. Form and content are intimately related: social consciousness and the desire to communicate with the masses demand a direct, forceful form of expression. Celaya criticizes the formalistic poetry of the postwar Garcilasists—"La razón de la sin-razón" (The Reason for the Unreasonable), "Veinte años de poesía" (Twenty Years of Poetry), "Las cosas como son" (Things as They Are)—because it avoids confrontation with the injustice which plagues mankind; it is an irresponsible, cowardly escape into the fantastic world of aestheticism. Celaya here forfeits the perfect balance between content and form, stressed as necessary for artistic communication in *El arte como lenguaje,* in favor of content. He defends the use of ordinary language, saying that his works reflect reality which for him is not unpoetic but marvelous ("Carta abierta a Victoriano Crémer" [Open Letter from Victoriano Crémer]). Furthermore the reader, accustomed to the formalism of the Surrealists and Garcilasists, is surprised by the novelty of a more direct form of expression and thus better able to feel the poet's intuitions.

In one interesting section of *Poesía y verdad,* entitled "Las buenas formas," Celaya clarifies his reproach to the formalists, indicating that his criticism of them in no way means that he rejects the concept of poetic language. On the contrary, form is essential inasmuch as it helps in the communication of the poet's unique experience, avoiding the danger of becoming so individualistic that communication fails. Celaya addresses himself specifically to the question of rhythm and rhyme. An irregular, assonantal rhyme is as effective as one that follows the mechanical laws of rhyme established by formal poetic tradition. With respect to rhyme and other stylistic characteristics discussed in *Poesía y verdad,* it is apparent that Celaya's concepts of poetry tended toward those of the popular, oral tradition.

Exploración de la poesía investigates the works of Fernando de Herrera, Gustavo Adolfo Bécquer and San Juan de la Cruz (Saint John of the Cross). Celaya concludes that there are three essential kinds of poetry. The types described repeat themselves in the history of literature, and the particular authors selected are only representative examples. *Exploración de la poesía* is perhaps Celaya's most successful essay. Unity is achieved through careful construction, including a clearly defined contrast between Herrera and Bécquer and an original interpretation of the poetry of San Juan de la Cruz, which synthesizes that of the other two authors. The seventeenth-century poet Fernando de Herrera represents "pure" poetry. To construct a perfect poem, an object, a thing of beauty, is his goal. Poetry is language, and Herrera believes he must perfect the latter, discovering in the sounds of language the essential meaning of things. Herrera does not express his own personal feelings, for these could contaminate the perfect beauty of a poem, but rather he shapes reality to conform to his art, inventing platonic love affairs or mustering patriotic sentiment. Celaya judges that the extreme importance given to form and the creation of the image of beauty leads to verses in which spontaneity, freshness, and sincerity are lacking. Stéphane Mallarmé, a nineteenth-century French Symbolist poet, represents for Celaya a more recent manifestation of "pure" poetry. Referring both to Herrera and Mallarmé, Celaya concludes: "They have renounced living as men in order to live as authors. They are born of their own works; they sacrifice everything for their art. And the adventure of an 'I' throughout a sonnet or the resonances and shades of a vowel in a tercet are for them passionate and decisive events."[27]

For Gustavo Adolfo Bécquer, poetry exists independently of the written poem, somewhere in the beyond, in the world of the inexpressible, the subconscious. A poem is not an end in itself, as it is for Herrera, but a means of reaching toward Poetry where the mysteries of human existence are to be found. Bécquer's poems are an effort to capture some fleeting glimpse of the ineffable, to evoke some secret that will shed light on the essence of our existence. Inside Bécquer lives a double who is in contact with the mysterious, subconscious realm where a reality very distinct from the rational one we know exists. Bécquer struggles to give himself over to his double so that he might surpass the limitations of "self" and reach a sense of communion with the beyond.

Celaya explains how Bécquer's metapoetry results in a very different kind of poetic language than that of Herrera: "If, instead of communication, we are looking for communion, it is evident that above all we retreat from articulate language, appropriate for directed thought, and move toward the primordial 'sonorous gesture'—shouts, crys, sighs."[28] Through the use of images, Bécquer fills us with suggestions and resonances that belong to the life of our origins. The metapoetry of Bécquer, which Celaya carefully parallels with that of Arthur Rimbaud, has an inherent danger. If the poet is not capable of understanding or finding the words to express the voice of his double, he may retreat into silence or go insane in the struggle for expression.

In one sense it can be said that San Juan de La Cruz, like Bécquer, writes metapoetry because he leaves the limits of "self," searching for the mysterious realm of the secrets of life. Unlike Bécquer, who only attains fleeting moments of truth and continues to search for the ineffable, San Juan de la Cruz reaches his goal of communion with God. But this personal transcendence is not Saint John's final aim. He returns to the rational world with a desire to communicate his experience to others. His poetry combines the metapoetic experience of Bécquer and the artistic effort of Herrera, thereby expressing with precision his knowledge of the ineffable realm. Celaya summarizes, saying that for San Juan de la Cruz poetry was "a lesson, a mandate, or as we would say today, poetry of commitment."[29]

In *Inquisición de la poesía* many concepts are elaborations of those found in previous essays. *Inquisición de la poesía* might best be described as a defense of the poetry of reality. For Celaya, confronting reality means accepting the importance of social structures, both with regard to how they determine the type of poetry an author writes—this concept reflects the writings of Georg Lukacs—and what directions poetry must take in the future. From a reflective, theoretical point of view, Celaya is once again concerned with social poetry, perhaps attempting to clarify and justify certain aspects of his own works which have been misunderstood by "purist" critics. Celaya points out that all poetry, whether or not it contains themes of class injustice, is social in the sense that it involves the author, the listener, and their interaction. The first step in the defense of poetry of reality is to discredit the myth of poetic inspiration. Poetry is the result of experience, forgotten or submerged in the subconscious, which is somehow recalled by the poet. It is not visionary contact with the mysterious voices of the beyond as Bécquer, Rimbaud, and the Surrealists pretend. When poets strive for absolute language and fail to direct their poetry to a listener, it becomes a verbal fetish, hermetic, and lacking in its essential function of communication.

In harmony with the theory that poetry is communication, Celaya underlines the importance of certain stylistic devices characteristic of folk poetry, such as repetition and parallelism. Rhythm, as opposed to traditional meter, is a broader and older concept, including semantic intonation and breath pauses as well as tonic accents, and should be an acceptable means of describing a poem's musicality. Likewise, rhyme should not be thought of in the narrow, formal sense of appearing at the end of verses, but in a more general manner including all the internal interplay of vowel sounds. Celaya again emphasizes the necessity of surprise—achieved with such devices as exaggeration, contrast, ellipsis and original metaphors—for intensifying the reader's response. He also stresses the importance of prolonging the response, principally achieved, through repetition.

In *Inquisición de la poesía* Celaya also addresses the question of literary immortality, a topic not elaborated on in previous essays. Poetry is eternal, not as a finite, perfect artistic elaboration by one individual, but as a living creation, belonging to the "natural-historic" reality of mankind, recreated and relived by each new generation. Poetry fulfills its function only to the extent that the poet overcomes the limitations of "self" and reaches out to others, expressing their feelings as if they were his own. For Celaya, the disappearance of "self" and the birth of a voice which sings of the experience of others and of mankind is the essence of poetry. These concepts are a reiteration of those found in the narratives.

VI *Conclusions*

Celaya's prose writings shed light on his poetry, and also affirm the poet's creative vitality which cannot be contained in one genre. His prose experiments can be successful—for example, the narrative *Lo uno y lo otro* and the essay *Exploración de la poesía*. Celaya's narratives have a thematic monotone with long discourses repeating certain basic intuitions. This defect has a positive side, for Celaya, the thinker, the would-be philosopher, offers a more elaborate presentation of his ideas in the narratives, which can enrich the reader's understanding of his poetry. Celaya especially emphasizes a process of self-examination and renewal. A conflict in man's nature—the amorphous, chaotic, feminine forces opposed to the individual, active, masculine forces—must be resolved in a perfect balance if the renewal process is to be completed. Conflict is again seen as an essential characteristic of his work, here as part of his thoughts about human nature. In his literary essays, Celaya consistently upholds certain concepts, especially that poetry is communication and that a "surprising" language must be discovered by the poet to express himself effectively. Formalism for the sake of perfection and absolute beauty is never endorsed. Poetic modification of normal language should always be aimed at enhancing communication. Other concepts of poetry, including moral responsibility to deal with social injustice, are especially supported during the period of social poetry.

CHAPTER 7

Celaya's Contributions

C ELAYA played a vital role in giving new direction to Spanish
poetry after the Civil War. All his enthusiasm and determination to write the kind of poetry he felt he must, were needed to
overcome the conditions which opposed change. On the one hand,
political repression under Franco's dictatorship made it most
difficult, often impossible, to express any desire for social change or
to find fault with the regime. With respect to the literary situation,
"it is necessary to keep in mind, when proceeding to a historical
evaluation of the change which the postwar poets effected, that
more than sixty years of Symbolist tradition weighed on them, no
small pressure against any type of realist expression."[1] Celaya was
one of the most important voices in overcoming these pressures
against a poetry of reality.

In evaluating Celaya's contribution to Spanish poetry, however,
we cannot simply classify him as a historically opportune spokesman, or as a prosaic social poet, as do many critics. Careful study of
his works reveals a complex creative talent; his poetry evolves
through four distinct stages. Although not all of his works exhibit
great originality or excellence, there are some very successful
books—*Los poemas de Juan de Leceta* and *La higa de Arbigorriya*,
for example—which combine familiar, direct language and irony to
express with great intensity the poet's unique human insights.

The variety and complexity of Celaya's poetry become apparent
when we examine the general characteristics of each period.

1. 1934–1944. Two important trends are reflected in Celaya's
early poetry, a reminiscence of certain aspects of the poetry of Juan
Ramón Jiménez, and the strong influence of the Generation of 1927
at a time when these poets were adopting Surrealist techniques.
Although the poet deeply senses the anguish of his limited human
existence, there are often ecstatic moments reached through con-

templation, eroticism, union with the primitive beginnings of life, and aestheticism.

2. 1945–1954. Celaya moves away from formalism and individualistic, irrational metaphorical language to a simpler, more direct style using everyday language. The tone and themes are often reminiscent of the poetry of Miguel de Unamuno and Antonio Machado. Existential anguish predominates, but contrary feelings—love, and the collective hope of the brotherhood of mankind—are also expressed. Variations of techniques from the first period, together with the introduction of ironic and dramatic forms, are combined effectively to create a new tone of urgency and directness. The poetry of the second period includes some of the most successful written by Celaya.

3. 1954–1962. Social poetry, already introduced, becomes dominant. What were originally very profound personal feelings of love and compassion for mankind gradually become dogmatic political views. Celaya, however, continues to be a complex poet, and some of the books reflect an inner struggle, while others express the joys of a personal relationship of love. The direct style is continued and modified, becoming more forceful, and at times rhetorical and even prosaic. The most successful technique is the use of dramatic resources.

4. 1962–1977. Rejection of social poetry and new experimentation are characteristic. For the most part the poet relies on the stylistic techniques of the first and second periods as a basis for his experiments. He achieves the best result with his innovative use of irony of the absurd. There are moments in which Celaya expresses hope for humanity, but a pessimistic view predominates.

I *The Conflict Despair-Joy*

The variety of the poetry written during the four periods is based on equally divergent views about the meaning and significance of poetry. Celaya's ideas range from a belief that poetry is a form of *conocimiento* (acquisition of knowledge), accompanied by highly personal stylistic techniques to convey private insights, to a belief that poetry is the voice of the masses and should speak to them in a language close to that of everyday life. In view of these opposing views, diverse stylistic techniques, and the variety of themes, it might appear that Celaya's poetry lacks any unifying characteristics. But if we turn to the emotional tone, we find that the conflict despair-joy gives unity to his production over the years.

Feelings of anguish and an attempt to overcome them are not unique to Celaya's poetry, but fall within the mainstream of modern literature. The predicament of contemporary man has shaped the course of recent poetry. Without a system of beliefs to give meaning to life, many modern poets have searched for alternatives to despair. The Symbolists, in their quest to discover some truth to replace the ruins of a lost faith in Christianity, clung to the ideal of absolute beauty. In the early twentieth century, the Surrealists discovered a new mythology of love and faith in the social myth of human solidarity. These two promises are interwoven, since compassion for the humble masses is an extension of the theme of love. Even the Existentialist writers have proposed an alternative to their pungent despair: the dehumanized, compassionless beings created by Albert Camus, for example, are a protest against "despiritualization." These writers wish to renew the dignity of the human condition by recognizing both man's limitations and his freedoms.

Numerous twentieth-century Spanish poets have similarly searched for answers. Miguel de Unamuno and Antonio Machado, once left alone to face the nothingness produced by a loss of faith, painfully and honestly confronted their doubts. Unamuno struggled with various options but never found an acceptable one.[2] Love offered Machado temporary happiness and the possibility of leaving "the great Zero" of time and death, if only for a short while. Juan Ramón Jiménez reached a very personal solution, achieving a timeless moment, similar to a mystic union, during moments of poetic creation. Some members of the Generation of 1927 found refuge in ideal beauty. Others, especially Dámaso Alonso in *Hijos de la ira,* directly confronted the inner despair and external circumstances of suffering and death. Vicente Aleixandre, perhaps more than any other poet of his generation, moved from anguish to an alternative of hope and communion with his fellowmen, presented vividly in *Historia del corazón.* The post–Civil War poetry of Spain fits well within this modern trend, and is frequently described as a vacillation between a tone of anguish and some alternative of hope.[3] Celaya's poetry is representative of the postwar generation because it is characterized by these two contrasting tones.

The conflict despair-joy, clearly within the mainstream of modern poetry, appears to be the core element of Celaya's poetic personality. The desperation which comes from an awareness of man's limited and apparently meaningless temporal existence is found throughout his poetic production. Likewise, feelings of joy and peace—usually associated with the themes of love, man's collective existence, the acceptance of death, and living only in the present moment—also consistently reappear. Other attempts to escape despair, especially eroticism and a return to the elementary beginnings of life, fail to provide more than momentary and incomplete relief.

The poet's feelings of joy are intimately related to the contrary state of despair. For example, Celaya has explained how his joyous feeling of unity with all mankind originated in a sense of deep personal anguish. In a brief introduction to the prologue of *Paz y concierto* (1953), Celaya recognizes that a sense of communion with others saved him from desperate feelings of nothingness and nonbeing: "In 1952–53, fighting against a period of despair that threatened to submerge me in something worse than silence, I wrote a group of poems that was published with the title of *Paz y concierto*. In that very difficult period for me, to feel at one with others is what sustained me."[4] Similarly, a variation of the collective spirit, Basque regionalism, is used by Celaya as a means of escaping the anguish of temporal existence. Identity with a long-standing cultural tradition diminishes the fear of nonbeing after death. A feeling of being part of the Basque country, which continues century after century, assures Celaya that he will form part of a tradition even after his death, and gives him the peace of this form of immorality, as revealed in the following verses of "La lluvia es dulce" (Rain is Sweet) from *Baladas y decires vascos* (1965): "No volveré. No volverá. / Pero el hombre colectivo, tú y yo juntos / reinará" ("I will not return. He will not return. But the collective man, you and I together will reign," PC 1074).

Sharing his innermost self in a deep, lasting love relationship can also be interpreted as a way by which the poet surmounts the agony of existence. From 1949, beginning with *Las cosas como son*, Celaya dedicates numerous books and poems to Amparo, sometimes affectionately calling her Amparito or Amparitxu. The opening strophes of "A Amparito Gastón" (*Las cartas boca arriba*, 1951) offer a vivid example of how love is capable of conquering the poet's preoccupation with death and replacing it with a zestful desire to discover joy in every moment of life:

> Amparito, porque hoy vienes
> buscándome a todo abril,
> matinal, lanzo al espacio
> mi qui, que sí, quiriquí.
> ¡Cantar, cantar! ¿Para qué?
> Para nada. Porque sí.
> Para ser mundo en el mundo
> Porque me gusta existir.

Amparito, because today you come looking for me, completely April-like, morninglike, I launch my song into space, yes-song, yes-sir-ree song. To sing, to sing! For what reason? For no reason at all. Just because. To be world in the world. Because I like to exist. (PC 381)

In the narratives, and in some of the long dramatic poems, Celaya suggests that conflict is a basic element of human nature. Each individual must confront the struggle between the heroic, masculine forces which provide the drive to be active and creative, and the feminine forces whose attraction is a lethargic, sensuous life.

The conflict between these two contrary emotional states is the one constant in Celaya's works. A study of form confirms the essential role of conflict as a unifying element, for it plays a significant role in the transformation of conceptual language into poetic language. Conflict is especially important in the most successful techniques, those which best help Celaya to express both the complexity and uniqueness of his intuitions. In visionary metaphors and system breakage, the poetic effect is achieved through a clash between our logical, rational perception and an unexpected, often irrational presentation by the poet. In addition to using these techniques in his poetry, Celaya in his essays of literary criticism frequently emphasizes the necessity of surprise, or a form of expression which conflicts with our normal way of perceiving things, to achieve the fundamental goal of poetry which is communication. Irony creates a poetic effect because of the simultaneous expression of conflicting emotions, and is used effectively by Celaya to express feelings of despair. The core element of drama is conflict, and Celaya finds dramatic resources appropriate when a joyous outlook struggles to victory.

Compared with his fellow postwar poets, Celaya's discordant vision of life differs significantly from theirs. His joyous outlook is more resilient, enthusiastic, and renewable than that of the others. In spite of the terrible pressures which awareness of living in a given time and place can impose, Celaya struggles again and again to move from despair toward a positive world vision.

Notes and References

Chapter One

1. Luis Cernuda, *Estudios sobre poesía española contemporánea* (Madrid-Bogota, 1957), pp. 184–89.

2. Emilio Alarcos Llorach, *La poesía de Blas de Otero* (Salamanca, 1973), p. 19.

3. Douglass Marcel Rodgers, "A Study of the Poetry of José Hierro as a Representative Fusion of Major Trends of Contemporary Spanish Poetry" (Ph.D. Diss., University of Wisconsin, 1964), p. 73. Dámaso Alonso, in *Poetas españoles contemporáneos* (Madrid, 1958), pp. 366–80, established the meaning of *arraigada* (rooted in tradition and faith) and *desarraigada* (without belief in any explanation of the meaning of life) with respect to contemporary Spanish poetry.

4. Vicente Aleixandre, *Algunos caracteres de la nueva poesía española* (Madrid, 1955), p. 8.

5. See Emilio Alarcos Llorach, *"Hijos de la ira* en 1944," *Insula,* nos. 138–39 (May–June, 1958), p. 7.

6. *Antología consultada de la joven poesía española,* ed. Francisco Ribes (Santander, 1952).

7. Gabriel Celaya in ibid., pp. 46–47.

8. Eugenio de Nora in ibid., p. 152.

9. Luis López Anglada, *Panorama poético español (Historia y antología 1939–1964)* (Madrid, 1965), p. 122.

10. René Wellek and Austin Warren, *Theory of Literature* (New York, 1956), p. 24, use the following distinction: "We reject as poetry or label as mere rhetoric everything which persuades us to a definite outward action. Genuine poetry affects us more subtly."

11. See David Bary, "José Hierro's 'Para un esteta,'" *PMLA*, 83, no. 5 (Oct. 1968) 1347–52.

12. Gabriel Celaya in *Antología consultada,* p. 46.

13. See José María Castellet, *Un cuarto de siglo de poesía española (1939–1964)* (Barcelona, 1973), p. 83, and José Hierro in *Antología consultada,* pp. 105–6.

14. José Olivio Jiménez, "La nueva poesía española (1960-1970)," *Insula*, no. 288 (Nov., 1970), p. 1.

15. Gabriel Celaya, *Itinerario póetico* (Madrid, 1975), p. 14.

16. Gabriel Celaya, personal interview with author (Madrid, June 2, 1975).

17. *Itinerario póetico*, pp. 15-16.

18. Gabriel Celaya, personal interview with author.

19. Gabriel Celaya in an interview with Fernando Samaniego, "Celaya vuelve al combate," *Informaciones (Suplemento artes y letras)*, March 13, 1975, pp. 1-2.

20. *Itinerario póetico*, p. 15.

21. Ibid., p. 13.

22. Gabriel Celaya, in personal interview with author, stated that several portions of *Espisodios nacionales* are based on his own experiences.

23. Ibid.

24. Ibid.

25. Gabriel Celaya, interview with Fernando Samaniego, p. 2.

26. Gabriel Celaya, in personal interview with the author, emphasized León Felipe's role in this respect and Neruda's comment.

27. Gabriel Celaya, *Cien poemas de un amor* (Barcelona, 1971), p. 7.

28. Gabriel Celaya, personal interview with author.

29. Gabriel Celaya, personal letter to author (Madrid, Oct. 28, 1976).

Chapter Two

1. Following is a list of dates of composition of early books which fall within the first period, even though not published until years which would be included in Celaya's second and fourth periods: *Los poemas de Rafael Múgica* (1934); *La soledad cerrada* (1934-1935); *La múisca y la sangre* (1934-1936); *Avenidas* (1939); *Objetos poéticos* (1940-1941); *El principio sin fin* (1942-1944).

2. *Los poemas de Juan de Leceta* was written 1944-1946. In 1947 the second part only appeared, with the title of "Tranquilamente hablando." "Avisos de Juan de Leceta," the first part, was not published until 1950, appearing with "La música y la sangre" and "Protopoesía" in a book entitled *Deriva*. The complete original version was published in 1961. *Entreacto* was written between 1953 and 1954 but not published until 1957.

3. Following are titles of books which contain materials previously published or originally part of another work: "Protopoesía," one section of *Deriva* (1950), consists of poems from *Movimientos elementales* (1947) and from *El principio sin fin* (1949) not included in the original edition of these two works. *Vía muerta* (1954) is an early extract of *Entreacto* (1957). *Poesía urgente* (1961) contains published works, selected poems, *Lo demás es silencio* (1952), and the first edition of *Vías de aqua*. *Dos cantatas* (1963)

combines *Cantata en Aleixandre* (1959) and the previously unpublished *El derecho y el revés. Lo que faltaba* (1964) includes *La linterna sorda* (1964), *Música de baile*, and *Lo que faltaba*, the latter two both appearing for the first time. *Canto en lo mío* (1968) is a combination of *Rapsodia éuskara* (1961) and *Baladas y decires vascos* (1965). *Cien poemas de un amor* (1971) is a selection of previously published love poems. *Dirección prohibida* (1973) consists of *Las resistencias del diamante* (1957), a shortened version of *Episodios nacionales* (1962), "Cantata en Cuba," published in *Papeles de Son Armadans* (1969), and the first publication of "Poemas tachados," poems which over the years had been rejected by the Spanish censorship. The second edition of *Las cartas boca arriba* (1974) consists of the original *Las cartas boca arriba* (1951) and a second section, "Otras cartas," which includes similar poems that had appeared in four different books. The second edition of *Cantos íberos* (1975) combines *Cantos íberos* (1954) and selected poems of *Lo que faltaba* (1966). Celaya's anthologies, including French and Italian translations, all contain previously published works.

4. Gabriel Celaya, personal letter to the author (Madrid, Feb. 13, 1970): "Any differences between the first editions of individual books or parts of books with regard to groupings of poems and titles and the way they appear in *Poesías completas* (Madrid, 1968) are due to the demands of the original editors." Further references to *Poesías completas* will appear in the text as PC followed by the page numbers.

5. Doreste Ventura, "Las cosas como son," *Insula*, July 17, 1949, n.p.

6. Gabriel Celaya, personal interview with author (Madrid, June 2, 1975).

7. See Walpola Rahula, *What the Buddha Taught* (Bedford, 1959), pp. 71–72, for a description of the importance of the present moment in Buddhism.

8. Gabriel Celaya, "Notas para una 'Cantata en Aleixandre,'" *Papeles de Son Armadans*, no. 32 (Nov.–Dec., 1958), p. 355.

9. Carlos Bousoño, *Teoría de la expresión poética* (Madrid, 1952), p. 102.

10. J. M. Cohen, *Poetry of This Age: 1908–1965* (New York, 1966), p. 162.

11. See Gabriel Celaya, "La aventura poética," *Poesías completas* (Madrid, 1968), p. 972 for an explanation of the poet's use of irrational metaphorical techniques.

12. See Amado Alonso, *Poesía y estilo de Pablo Neruda* (Buenos Aires, 1968), pp. 54–55, and Paul Ilie, *The Surrealist Mode in Spanish Literature* (Ann Arbor, 1968), p. 127, for descriptions of how irrational metaphorical techniques clash with our normal use of language.

13. *Teoría de la expresión poética*, p. 96.

14. Ibid.

15. See Carlos Ramos-Gil, *Claves líricas de García Lorca* (Madrid, 1967) for the use of symbols in the poetry of Federico García Lorca.

16. Carlos Bousoño, *Teoría de la expresión poética*, p. 223. The types of system breakage described in this section follow those outlined by Bousoño in chapter 11, pp. 222–93.

17. Leo Spitzer, *La enumeración caótica en la poesía moderna*, trans. Raimundo Lida (Buenos Aires, 1945).

18. Gabriel Celaya, in a personal interview with the author, named *La soledad cerrada* as the most representative book of the first period.

Chapter Three

1. In an interview (Madrid, June 2, 1975) the following exchange occurred: Celaya: "It is precisely the period 1945–1946 when I began to open up." Ugalde: "Did you read Sartre?" Celaya: "Yes. There is a great deal of influence of Sartre in my work, a very great amount of Sartre. It's evident, isn't it?"

2. Gabriel Celaya, interview on the television program "Directísmo" (Madrid, December 20, 1975).

3. See Vicente Gaos, *Prosa fugitiva: entrevista* (Madrid, 1975), pp. 60–61, for a statement of Celaya regarding his very high opinion of the poetry of Neruda.

4. See Gabriel Celaya, "Introduction," *Itinerario poético* (Madrid, 1975), p. 23.

5. See Antonio Sánchez Barbudo, *Los poemas de Antonio Machado. Los temas. El sentimiento y la expresión.* (Madison, 1969), p. 436.

6. Dámaso Alonso, *Poetas españoles contemporáneos* (Madrid, 1965), p. 173.

7. Gabriel Celaya, *Inquisición de la poesía* (Madrid, 1972), p. 100.

8. Gabriel Celaya, *Poesía y verdad* (Pontevedra, 1954), p. 38.

9. Vicente Aleixandre, *Algunos caracteres de la nueva poesía espãnola* (Madrid, 1955), pp. 25–26, emphasizes the narrative quality of post–Civil War poetry.

10. Alan Reynolds Thompson, *The Dry Mock. A Study of Irony in Drama* (Berkeley, 1948), p. 11.

11. Ibid., p. 5.

12. David Worcester, *The Art of Satire* (Cambridge, 1940), p. 88.

13. Alan Reynolds Thompson, *The Dry Mock*, p. 7.

14. Ibid., p. 9.

15. David Worcester, *The Art of Satire*, p. 128.

16. See Charles I. Glicksberg, *The Ironic Vision in Modern Literature* (The Hague, 1969).

17. David Worcester, *The Art of Satire*, p. 106.

18. José Hierro, "*Entreacto* de Gabriel Celaya," *Poesía española*, no. 77 (December, 1957), p. 9.

Chapter Four

1. Paul Ilie, "The Disguises of Protest: Contemporary Spanish Poetry," *The Michigan Quarterly Review*, 10, no. 1 (Winter, 1971), 38–48.

2. Gabriel Celaya in *Antología consultada*, ed. Francisco Ribes (Valencia, 1952), p. 44.

3. See Max Aub, *Una nueva poesía española 1950–55* Mexico, 1957) and J. M. Navarro, "La nueva poesía española," *Revista Nacional de Cultura*, Caracas, nos. 156–57 (1963), pp. 110–19.

4. Archibald MacLeish, "Poetry and the Public World," *A Time to Speak, The Selected Prose of Archibald MacLeish* (Boston, 1952), p. 88.

5. María Zambrano, "Poesía y revolución: *El Hombre y el trabajo* de Arturo Serrano-Plaja," *Hora de España*, no. 18 (June, 1939), p. 52.

6. Gabriel Celaya, "Notas para una 'Cantata en Aleixandre,' " *Papeles de Son Armadans*, no. 32 (November–December, 1958), pp. 375–85.

7. In ibid., p. 383, Celaya summarizes the nature of the different characters.

8. Gabriel Celaya, *Itinerario poético* (Madrid, 1975), p. 29.

9. Gabriel Celaya, "Nota," in *Poesía urgente* (Buenos-Aires, 1960), p. 7.

10. Ramón de Garcíasol, "Poesía y pueblo," *Insula*, nos. 200–201 (July–August, 1963), p. 5.

11. Pablo Vives, "Gabriel Celaya," *Les Lettres Francaises*, no. 828 (May 24–30, 1962), p. 4.

12. Miguel Fernández, "Gabriel Celaya, uno de los primeros promotores de la 'poesía social,' " *España*, Tanger, September 30, 1965, p. 3.

13. Guillermo Díaz-Plaja, *La creación literaria en España, Primera bienal de crítica* (Madrid, 1968), p. 32.

14. For further information on the *caballeritos* see Luis Pena Basurto and others, *Los Caballeritos de Azcoitia* (San Sebastián, 1963).

15. Douglass Marcel Rodgers, "A Study of the Poetry of José Hierro as a Representative Fusion of Major Trends of Contemporary Spanish Poetry" (Ph.D. Diss., University of Wisconsin, 1964), p. 106, emphasizes the disparity between pronouncements and poetry in several postwar poets. See also David Bary, "José Hierro's 'para un estata,' " *PMLA* 83, no. 5 (Oct. 1968), 1347–52 for a description of a similar discrepancy between Hierro's statements of poetic theory and his poems.

16. José Hierro, "*Entreacto* de Gabriel Celaya," *Poesía Española* (December, 1957), p. 8.

17. See Manuel Mantero, "Gabriel Celaya: *Para vosotros dos*," *Agora*, nos. 49–50 (November–December, 1960), p. 58.

18. Gabriel Celaya, personal interview with author (Madrid, June 2, 1975) stated that *La buena vida*, originally conceived as a narrative to be called *Lázaro anda*, is the continuation of *Lázaro calla*, a narrative published in 1949.

19. Gabriel Celaya, "Carta abierta a Carlos Murciano," *Insula*, no. 180

(November, 1961), p. 3, describes the conflicting forces represented by the characters.

20. See for example, Rafael Bosch, "Gabriel Celaya, *La buena vida*," *Books Abroad* 37, no. 1 (Winter, 1963), 63.

21. The content of the long poems from the second period is described in chapter 3 of this text. For a detailed analysis of the dramatic structure of *Las cosas como son* see Sharon E. Ugalde, "Los recursos dramáticos en la poesía de Gabriel Celaya," *Papeles de Son Armadans*, nos. 233–34 (August–September, 1975), 109–42.

22. See Gustav Freytag, "The Techniques of Drama," Ferdinand Brunetière, "The Law of Drama," and William Archer, "Brunetière's Law," in *European Theories of the Drama*, ed. Barret H. Clark (Cincinnati, 1918), pp. 345, 403, 407.

23. Brander Mathews, "Notes to the English Translation of Brunetière's Law of Drama," in *European Theories of the Drama*, p. 403.

24. Marian Gallaway, *Constructing a Play* (New York, 1950), p. 259.

25. See George Pierce Baker, *Dramatic Techniques* (New York, 1919), p. 213.

26. Marian Gallaway, *Constructing a Play*, p. 189.

27. Ibid., pp. 46–64.

28. Javier Alfaya, "*Dos cantatas* de Gabriel Celaya," *Insula*, no. 221 (April, 1965), p. 7.

29. Leopoldo de Luis, "Dos cantatas de Gabriel Celaya," *Papels de son Armadans*, no. 97 (May, 1964), pp. 233–36.

30. Ferdinand Brunetière, "The Law of Drama," p. 410.

31. Alan Reynolds Thompson, *The Anatomy of Drama* (Berkeley, 1946), p. 121.

32. Gabriel Celaya, "Carta abierta a Carlos Murciano," explains that his long dramatic poems are not dramas *per se*.

33. Alan Reynolds Thompson, *The Dry Mock*, p. 410, describes dramas with a high degree of detachment.

34. Rafael Bosch, "Gabriel Celaya, *La buena vida*," p. 63.

35. See Juan Luis Alborg, *Historia de la literatura española* (Madrid, 1967), II, 713–22 for a more complete description of the *auto* and its origin.

36. Angel Valbuena Prat, "Prólogo," in *Autos sacramentales II*, by Calderón de la Barca (Madrid, 1927), pp. lxxi–lxxvii.

37. Zelda Irene Brooks, "Major Themes in the Poetry of Gabriel Celaya" (Ph.D. Diss., University of Oklahoma, 1968), p. 95.

38. M. C. Bradbrook, *English Dramatic Form: A History of its Development* (New York, 1965), p. 152 describes the relationship between the moralities and political drama of the 1920s and 1930s.

39. Robert Marrast, *Aspects du Theatre de Rafael Alberti* (Paris, 1967), p. 31, and Juan Cano Ballesta, "La renovación poética de los treinta y Miguel Hernández," *Symposium* (Summer, 1968), pp. 123–31, both stress the influence of the *auto*.

40. Friedrich Von Schiller, "On Tragic Art," in *European Theories of the Drama*, p. 320.

41. See Andrew P. Debicki, *Estudios sobre poesía española contemporánea, La generación de 1924–1925* (Madrid, 1968), pp. 234–43.

42. August Wilhelm Schlegel, "Lectures on Dramatic Art and Literature," in *European Theories of the Drama*, p. 340.

43. Ramón Menéndez-Pidal, *Romancero hispánico (hispano-portugués, americano y sefardí), Teoría e historia* (Madrid, 1953), I, 60.

44. Juan Luis Alborg, *Historia de la literatura española*, p. 130.

45. Manuel Muñoz Cortés, "Gabriel Celaya y Juan de Leceta: *Las cosas como son*," *Arriba*, April 24, 1949, p. 3, and David Bary, "Sobre el nombrar poético en la poesía española contemporánea," *Papeles de Son Armadans*, no. 44 (February, 1957), 161–89, stress the importance of contrasting styles in Celaya's poetry.

Chapter Five

1. Gabriel Celaya, "Introducción," *Itinerario poético* (Madrid, 1975), p. 28.

2. See Luis Jiménez Martos, "Gabriel Celaya: *Mazorcas*," *La estafeta literaria*, no. 245 (1962), p. 18.

3. Jorge Guillén, "Introduction," *Cántico: A Selection*, ed. Norman Thomas DiGiovanni (Boston, 1965), p. 9. See also Vicente Gaos, *Prosa fugitiva: Entrevistas* (Madrid, 1955), pp. 60–61, in which Celaya affirms his admiration for Guillén.

4. See Rafel Bosch, "Gabriel Celaya: *Mazorcas*," *Books Abroad* 37, no. 3 (Summer, 1963), 318.

5. Ramón Barce, "Escaparate de la poesía: *Versos de otoño* por Gabriel Celaya," *Ya*, December 19, 1965, n.p.

6. Gabriel Celaya, personal interview with author (Madrid: June 2, 1975), stated that this book is incidental to the mainstream of his production and that he was inspired to write it because at that time he frequented jazz clubs in the company of Amparo Gastón and fellow poet Angel González.

7. Charles I. Glicksberg, *The Ironic Vision in Modern Literature* (The Hague, 1969), p. 228.

8. L. A. Murillo, *The Cyclical Night: Irony in James Joyce and Jorge Luis Borges* (Cambridge, 1968), p. xvii, describes how complex irony techniques can call attention to themselves and thus alter the content. This process is at work in some of Celaya's poems.

9. Gabriel Celaya, *Lírica de cámara* (Barcelona, 1969), p. 57. Other references to this book will be noted in the text as LC followed by page number.

10. Gabriel Celaya, *Operaciones poéticas* (Madrid, 1971), p. 13. Other references to this book will be noted in the text as OP followed by page number.

11. See Gabriel Celaya, "Fin de la tragedia," *Función de Uno, Equis, Ene* (Zaragoza, 1973), pp. 46–47.

12. Gabriel Celaya, personal interview with author.

13. Ibid.

14. Gabriel Celaya, "Sí, no, sí," *La higa de Arbigorriya* (Madrid, 1975), p. 89. Other references to this book will be noted in the text as HA followed by page number.

15. Gabriel Celaya, "No la justicia, la paz," *Buenos días, buenas noches* (Pamplona, 1976), p. 22.

Chapter Six

1. Gabriel Celaya, personal interview with author (Madrid, June 2, 1975).

2. See Frank Everette Rosemond, "Gabriel Celaya: Peregrinación metafísica a través de su prosa" (Ph.D. Diss., University of New Mexico, 1971), pp. vi–vii, for a description of the renewal process.

3. Gabriel Celaya, personal interview with author.

4. Ibid.

5. See Frank Everette Rosemond, "Gabriel Celaya," who interviewed Celaya regarding these similarities with Nietzsche, p. 7.

6. Ibid., p. 11, points out the influence of Jung and Freud.

7. Gabriel Celaya, "Introducción," *Itinerario poético* (Madrid, 1975), p. 20.

8. Gabriel Celaya, *Tentativas*, 2nd ed. (Barcelona, 1972), p. 129.

9. Gabriel Celaya, personal interview with the author.

10. Gabriel Celaya, *Lázaro calla*, 2nd ed. (Madrid, 1974), pp. 25–26.

11. Ibid., p. 101.

12. Ibid., p. 172.

13. See Mircea Eliade, *The Myth of the Eternal Return*, trans. Willard R. Trask (New York, 1954). Celaya's concept of the cyclical repetition of phases of mankind is very similar to the myth of the eternal return described by Eliade.

14. Gabriel Celaya, *Penúltimas tentativas* (Madrid, 1960), pp. 92–93.

15. Ibid., p. 147.

16. Ibid., p. 96.

17. Gabriel Celaya, *Lo uno y lo otro* (Barcelona, 1962), p. 23.

18. Frank Everette Rosemond, "Gabriel Celaya," p. 99, carefully analyzes the relationship between the Existential content and the detective-story structure.

19. Gabriel Celaya, *Los buenos negocios* (Barcelona, 1962), p. 73.

20. Frank Everette Rosemond, p. 71.

21. José Domingo, "Crónica de Novela: Vargas Llosa, Gabriel Celaya," *Insula*, no. 235 (June, 1966), p. 3.

22. P. Vila San-Juan, "Informaciones teatrales y cinematográficas," *ABC* (Madrid) March 1, 1973, p. 79.

23. Gabriel Celaya, *El arte como lenguaje* (Bilbao, 1951), p. 28.

24. Ibid., p. 45.

25. Ibid., p. 17.

26. Gabriei Celaya, "Respuesta a *El Correo Literario*," in *Poesía y verdad* (Pontevedra, 1960), p. 69.

27. Gabriel Celaya, *Exploración de la poesía*, 2nd ed. (Barcelona, 1971), p. 42.

28. Ibid., p. 120.

29. Ibid., p. 192.

Chapter Seven

1. José María Castellet, *Un cuarto de siglo de poesía española (1939–1964)* (Barcelona, 1973), p. 95.

2. See Concha Zardoya, "Los caminos poéticos del '98" in *Poesía española del '98 y del '27* (Madrid, 1968) for a discussion of the various "ways" or alternatives attempted by Unamuno.

3. See, for example, Vicente Aleixandre, *Algunos caracteres de la nueva poesía española* (Madrid, 1955), p. 5; Caballero Bonald, "Apostillas a la generación poética del '36," *Insula*, nos. 224–25 (July–August, 1965), p. 5; and Rafael Bosch, "La nueva poesía inconfromista española," *Hispania* 46 (1963), pp. 71–76.

4. Gabriel Celaya, "Nadie es nadie," in *Poesía y verdad* (Pontevedra, 1960), p. 78.

Selected Bibliography

PRIMARY SOURCES

1. Poetry

Marea del silencio. Zarauz: Itxaropena, 1935.
La soledad cerrada (includes *Vuelo Perdido*). San Sebastián: Norte, 1947.
Movimientos elementales. San Sebastián: Norte, 1947.
Tranquilamente hablando. San Sebastián: Norte, 1947.
Objetos poéticos. Valladolid: Halcón, 1948.
El principio sin fin. Córdoba: Cántico, 1949.
Se parece al amor. Las Palmas: El Arca Cerrada, 1949.
Las cosas como son. Santander: La Isla de los Ratones, 1949. 2d ed. 1952.
Deriva (includes *La música y la sangre, Protopoesía, Avisos*). Alicante: Ifach, 1950.
Las cartas boca arriba. Madrid: Adonais, 1951. 2d ed. Madrid: Turner, 1974.
Lo demás es silencio. Barcelona: El Cucuyo, 1952.
Paz y concierto. Madrid: El Pájaro de Paja, 1953.
Vía muerta. Barcelona: Alcor, 1954.
Cantos íberos. Alicante: Verbo, 1955. 2d ed. Madrid: Turner, 1975.
De claro en claro. Madrid: Adonais, 1956.
Pequeña antología poética. Santander: Cigarra, 1957.
Entreacto. Madrid: Agora, 1957.
Las resistencias del diamante. Mexico: Libros Luciérnaga, 1957. 2d ed. (bilingual). *L'irreductible diamant.* Paris-Marseilles: Action Poétique, 1960.
Cantata en Aleixandre. Madrid-Palma: Papeles de Son Armadans, 1959.
El corazón en su sitio. Caracas: Lírica Hispana, 1959.
Para vosotros dos. Bilbao: Alrededor de la Mesa, 1960.
Poesía urgente (includes *Poesía directa, Lo demás es silencio, Vías de agua*). Buenos Aires: Losada, 1960. 2d ed. 1972.
La buena vida. Santander: La Isla de los Ratones, 1961.

Los poemas de Juan Leceta (includes *Avisos, Tranquilamente hablando, Las cosas como son*). Barcelona: Colliure, 1961.

Rapsodia éuskara. San Sebastián: Biblioteca Vascongada de los Amigos del País, 1961.

L'Espagne en marche (bilingual anthology). Paris: Seghers, 1961.

Episodios nacionales. París: Ruedo Ibérico, 1962.

Poesía (1934–1961). Madrid: Giner, 1962.

Mazorcas. Palencia: Rocamador, 1962.

Versos de otoño. Jerez de la Frontera: La Venecia, 1963.

Dos cantatas (includes *Cantata en Aleixandre* and *El derecho y el revés*). Madrid: Revista de Occidente, 1964. 2d ed. Madrid: Turner, 1976.

La linterna sorda. Barcelona: El Bardo, 1964.

Baladas y decires vascos. Barcelona: El Bardo, 1965.

Lo que faltaba (includes *La linterna sorda* and *Música de baile*). Barcelona: El Bardo, 1967.

Poemas de Rafael Múgica. Bilbao: Comunicación Literaria de Autores, 1967.

Poesie (bilingual anthology). Milan: Arnoldo Mondadori, 1967.

Los espejos transparentes. Barcelona: El Bardo, 1968. 2d ed. 1969.

Canto en lo mío (includes *Rapsodia éuskara* and *Baladas y decires vascos*). Barcelona: El Bardo, 1968. 2d ed. San Sebastián: Auñamendi, 1973.

Poesías completas. Madrid: Aguilar, 1969.

Lírica de cámara. Barcelona: El Bardo, 1969.

Operaciones poéticas. Madrid: Visor, 1971.

Cien poemas de un amor. Barcelona: Plaza y Janés, 1971. 2d ed., 1974.

Campos semánticos. Zaragoza: Javalambre, 1971.

Dirección prohibida (includes *Las resistencias del diamante, Poemas tachados, Episodios nacionales, Cantata en Cuba*). Buenos Aires: Losada, 1973.

Función de Uno, Equis, Ene. Zaragoza: Fuendetodos, 1973.

El derecho y el revés. Barcelona: Ocnos, 1973.

Itinerario poético. Madrid: Cátedra, 1975.

La higa de Arbigorriya. Madrid: Visor, 1975.

Buenos días, buenas noches. Pamplona: I. Peralta, 1976.

2. Poetry in Collaboration with Amparo Gastón

Ciento volando. Madrid: Neblí, 1953.

Coser y cantar. Guadalajara: Doña Endrina, 1955.

Música celestial. Cartagena: Baladre, 1958.

3. Narratives

Tentativas. Madrid: Adán, 1946.

Lázaro calla. Madrid: S.G.E. de L., 1949. 2d ed. Madrid: Júcar, 1972.

Penúltimas tentativas. Madrid: Arión, 1960.
Lo uno y lo otro. Barcelona: Seix Barral, 1962.
Los buenos negocios. Barcelona: Seix Barral, 1965.

4. Essays

El arte como lenguaje. Bilbao: Conferencias y Ensayos, 1951.
Poesía y verdad. Pontevedra: Huguin, 1960.
Exploración de la poesía. Barcelona: Seix Barral, 1964. 2d ed. 1971.
Inquisición de la poesía. Madrid: Taurus, 1972.
La voz de los niños. Barcelona: Laia, 1972.
Bécquer. Madrid: Júcar, 1972.

5. Drama

El Revelo. San Sebastián: Gora, 1963. 2d ed. Madrid: Escelicer, 1972.

6. Translations

Rainer Maria Rilke. *Cincuenta poemas franceses.* San Sebastián: Norte, 1947.
William Blake. *El libro de Urizen.* San Sebastián: Norte, 1947.
Jean Arthur Rimbaud. *Una temporada en el infierno.* San Sebastián: Norte, 1947. 2d ed. Madrid: Visor, 1969. 3d ed. Visor, 1972.
Paul Éluard. *Quince poemas.* Guadalajara: Doña Endrina, 1954.

7. Selected Articles

"La obra de Juan Ramón Jiménez." *La Voz de España*, San Sebastián, April 13, 1948. p. 6.
"Existencialismo." *La Voz de España*, San Sebastián, June 5, 1948, p. 7.
"Notas para una 'Cantata de Aleixandre.' " *Papeles de Son Armadans*, no. 32 (Nov.–Dec. 1958), pp. 375–85.
"Cincuentenario de la Residencia de Estudiantes." *Insula*, no. 169 (Dec., 1960), p. 4.
"Rafael Múgica, Gabriel Celaya y Juan de Leceta." *Poesía de España*, no. 1 (1960), pp. 5–8.
"Tirios y troyanos (Sobre poesía y política)." *Insula*, no. 184 (March, 1962), p. 7.
"La poesía oral." *Revista de Occidente*, no. 23 (Feb., 1965), pp. 208–15.
"Mesa redonda sobre poesía," *Cuadernos para el diálogo*, Special Issue, No. 23 (Dec. 1970), 53–60.
"Pablo Neruda: Poeta del tercer día de la Creación," *Revista de Occidente*, No. 107 (Jan. 1972), 95–101.

154   GABRIEL CELAYA

SECONDARY SOURCES

ALEIXANDRE, VICENTE. *Algunos caracteres de la nueva poesía española.*
Madrid: Instituto de España, 1955. Excellent essay on postwar poetry;
emphasizes unifying characteristics of the writers.
ALONSO, DÁMASO. *Poetas españoles contemporáneos,* 3d ed. Madrid: Gre-
dos, 1965. Source material for Celaya's precursors (Generations of 1898
and 1927).
Antología consultada de la joven poesía española. Edited by Francisco
Ribes. Valencia: Mares, 1952. Contains poems and declarations of the
first group of postwar poets.
BARY, DAVID. "Sobre el nombrar poético en la poesía española contem-
poránea." *Papeles de Son Armadans,* no. 44 (Feb., 1957), 161–89.
Analyzes the technique of "contrasting styles" in selected postwar
poets.
BOUSOÑO, CARLOS. *Teoría de la expresión literaria.* Madrid: Gredos, 1952.
Contains extremely helpful descriptions of types of stylistic analysis.
BOWRA, C. M. *Poetry and Politics: 1900–1960.* Cambridge: Cambridge
University Press, 1966. Very useful for understanding how the social
poetry of Spain relates to similar tendencies elsewhere in Europe and
in Latin America.
———. *The Creative Experiment.* London: Macmillan, 1949. Excellent
background on the nature of post-Symbolist poetry.
BROOKS, ZELDA IRENE. "Major Themes in the Poetry of Gabriel Celaya."
Ph.D. Diss., University of Oklahoma, 1968. Deficient in some respects
but one of the few works which attempts to categorize and discuss
themes of Celaya's overall production.
CABALLERO BONALD, F. M. "Gabriel Celaya: *Poesía (1934–1961)." Insula,*
no. 190 (Sept., 1962), p. 5. In a brief review of the anthology, summarizes some of the important changes Celaya's poetry has undergone
during the years.
CANO, JOSÉ LUIS. *Poesía española del siglo XX.* Madrid: Guadarrama,
1960. *Las cartas boca arriba* discussed as characteristic of Celaya's
work. *Cantata en Aleixandre* described.
CASTELLET, JOSÉ MARÍA. "Prologue" to *Un cuarto de siglo de poesía española (1939–1964),* 6th ed. Barcelona: Seix Barral, 1973. Excellent
analysis of the development and nature of the "poetry of reality" of the
postwar years.
COHEN, J. M. *Poetry of This Age: 1908–1965.* New York: Harper and Row,
1966. Helpful overview of twentieth-century poetry, including important Spanish poets.
———. "Since the Civil War. New Currents in Spanish Poetry." *Encounter,* 12, no. 2 (Feb., 1959), 44–53. Treats individually several
members of the first generation of postwar poets, including Celaya.

DEBICKI, ANDREW P. *Estudios sobre poesía española contemporánea. La generación de 1924–1925.* Madrid: Gredos, 1968. Excellent source material for some of Celaya's precursors (often called Generation of 1927).

DOMENECH, RICARDO. "Entrevista con Gabriel Celaya." *Insula*, no. 199 (July 1963), p. 4. Celaya recognizes limitations of being the "voice of the masses."

FERRERO, ROSANA AND JUAN SANTISO. "Gabriel Celaya." *Pueblo*, Sept. 11, 1974, last page. Interview: reflections on his early days as a writer; importance of García Lorca, A. Machado, and M. Hernández for contemporary poetry stressed.

GALLAWAY, MARIAN. *Constructing a Play.* New York: Prentice Hall, 1950. Background for dramatic techniques useful in analyzing Celaya's poetry.

GAOS, VICENTE. "La revelación de Gabriel Celaya." *Prosa fugitiva: entrevistas.* Madrid: Colenda, 1955. An interview containing useful information regarding poets who have influenced Celaya.

GONZÁLEZ MARTIN, J. P. *Poesía hispánica, 1939–1969 (Estudio y Antología).* Barcelona: El Bardo, 1970. Presents conclusions regarding the evolution of Celaya's poetry.

GONZÁLEZ, ANGEL, "Introducción," Gabriel Celaya Poesía. Madrid: Alianza, 1977, pp. 7–30. Very helpful. One of the few articles which gives an overview of Celaya's poetry.

HIERRO, JOSÉ. "*Entreacto* de Gabriel Celaya." *Poesía española*, no. 77 (Dec., 1957), p. 9. Includes background on Celaya's conflict between "public" and "private" poetry.

JIMÉNEZ MARTOS, LUIS. "*Entreacto:* Gabriel Celaya." *Agora*, nos. 7–8 (1957), pp. 37–38. Points out Celaya's capacity to overcome anguish and express joyous feelings.

LÓPEZ, FRANÇOIS. "La Póesie de Gabriel Celaya." *Les Lettres françaises*, no. 900 (Nov. 15, 1961), p. 3. Begins with brief summary of prewar poetic atmosphere and description of Celaya's evolution.

LUIS, LEOPOLDO DE. "Primera suma poética de Gabriel Celaya." *Revista de Occidente*, no. 87 (June, 1970), pp. 319–27. Outlines Celaya's evolution and certain conflicts inherent in his poetry.

MANTERO, MANUEL. *Poesía española contemporánea: Estudio y antología (1939–1965).* Buenos Aires: Plaza y Jarnés, 1966. Studies different groups; includes section on Celaya emphasizing the variety of his production.

NICOLL, ALLARDYCE. *The Theory of Drama.* 3d ed. New York: Benjamin Blom, 1966. Background information for the study of Celaya's use of dramatic techniques.

OLIVIO JIMÉNEZ, JOSÉ. *Diez años de poesía española (1960–1970).* Madrid: Insula, 1972. Many references to Celaya's generation and the Generation of 1927 while principally describing the second group of postwar poets.

RAFFUCCI DE LOCKWOOD, ALACIA MARÍA. "Cuarto poetas de la Generacion del '36." Ph.D. Diss., University of Wisconsin, 1967. Thorough study of the Generation of 1936, especially M. Hernández, A. Serrano-Plaja, L. Panero, and L. Rosales, with a brief section on Celaya.

RODGERS, DOUGLASS MARCEL. "A Study of the Poetry of José Hierro as a Representative Fusion of Major Trends of Contemporary Spanish Poetry." Ph.D. Diss., University of Wisconsin, 1964. Contains a very good study of the development of postwar poetry.

ROSEMOND, FRANK EVERETTE. "Gabriel Celaya: Peregrinación metafísica a través de su prosa." Ph.D. Diss., University of New Mexico, 1971. Excellent study of the content and form of Celaya's narratives.

SEIRRA, PIERRE-OLIVIER. Gabriel Celaya. Paris: Seghers, 1970. Contains comprehensive presentation of Celaya's biography, poetic evolution, and an anthology.

SIEBENMANN, GUSTAV. Los estilos poéticos en España desde 1900. Madrid: Gredos, 1973. Superior source material on twentieth-century Spanish poetry. Ample material on postwar trends with several references to Celaya.

SOBEJANO, GONZALO. "Un análisis estilístico de la poesía de Miguel Hernández." Revista Hispánica Moderna, nos. 3–4 (July–October, 1963), pp. 305–6. Underlines importance of César Vallejo's influence on M. Hernández and others, including Celaya.

THOMPSON, ALAN REYNOLDS. The Dry Mock: A Study of Irony in Drama. Berkeley: University of California Press, 1948. Background information for the study of irony in Celaya's poetry.

TORRE, GUILLERMO DE LA. "Contemporary Spanish Poetry." Texas Quarterly 4, no. 1 (Spring, 1961), 55–78. Discusses poetry of commitment and differences between Celaya's proclamations and some of his poetry.

TORRENTE BALLESTER, GONZALO. Panorama de la literatura española. Madrid: Guadarrama, 1956. Points out inherent complexities of Celaya's apparently simple, straightforward style.

UGALDE, SHARON E. "Los recursos dramáticos en la poesía de Gabriel Celaya." Papeles de Son Armadans, no. 133–34 (Aug.–Sept., 1975), 109–42. Contains additional detailed examples of Celaya's use of dramatic structure.

VIVES, PABLO. "Gabriel Celaya." Les Lettres françaises, no. 828 (May 24–30, 1962), p. 4. Frank confessions by Celaya regarding disillusionment with social poetry.

VILA SAN-JUAN, P. "El Revelo, de Gabriel Celaya, en el Club Pueblo." ABC, March 1, 1973, p. 79. Analysis of drama and comments on public's reaction to it.

YRACHE, LUIS. "Una excursión de Gabriel Celaya." *Papeles de Son Armadans*, no. 109 (April, 1965), pp. 106–12. Analysis of *La linterna sorda*.
ZARDOYA, CONCHA. *Poesía española del '98 y del '27*. Madrid: Gredos, 1968. Presents themes of the poets as alternatives to despair, closely related to content of some of Celaya's poetry.

Index